Contents

The Chicago Conspiracy Trial: A Short Narrative

The trial of political activists accused of inciting riots during the Democratic National Convention of 1968 attracted national attention and exposed the depths of political and cultural divisions at a crucial moment in the nation's history. The trial of the "Chicago Seven" became a defining event in public debates about the Vietnam War, the student protest movement, and the fairness of the federal judicial process.

The defendants and their lawyers used the courtroom as a platform for a broad critique of American society and an almost anarchic challenge to the legitimacy of governmental authority. The judge in the case displayed open contempt for the defendants, and his own unorthodox behavior threatened public confidence in the judiciary. The nearly five-month long trial illustrated the contentious and often theatrical nature of public affairs during the late 1960s and early 1970s.

Planning for the Democratic National Convention of 1968

In the fall of 1967, the Democratic Party decided to hold its 1968 national convention and the expected renomination of President Lyndon Johnson in Chicago. Mayor Richard Daley promised his city would be free of the civil disorders that had broken out in major cities in recent summers. By the summer of 1968, the prospects for a smooth convention had vanished. Johnson, in the face of growing protests against the Vietnam War and after assessing the surprising strength of Eugene McCarthy's campaign for President, withdrew in March from the race for the nomination. The assassination of Martin Luther King in April provoked devastating urban riots in Chicago and other cities. The assassination of Robert Kennedy in June further shocked the nation and complicated the race for the Democratic nomination. The spring of 1968 had also brought the Tet offensive against American forces in Vietnam and unprecedented student protests on university campuses. By August, many Americans believed the nation was in the midst of a profound political and cultural crisis.

Organizing protests at the Democratic convention

In the fall of 1967, members of the National Mobilization Committee to End the War in Vietnam proposed a massive anti-war demonstration to coincide with the expected renomination of President Johnson in Chicago. The National Mobilization Committee was directed by David Dellinger, a long-time pacifist, who had organized the march on the Pentagon in October 1967. In early 1968, the National Mobilization

1

opened a Chicago office directed by Rennie Davis and Tom Hayden, who were leading political organizers and former leaders of Students for a Democratic Society.

A small group of cultural radicals, including Jerry Rubin, who helped Dellinger organize the march on the Pentagon, and Abbie Hoffman, an organizer of political theater events, planned a "Festival of Life" to counter the Democratic "Convention of Death." Rubin and Hoffman dubbed themselves the Yippie movement, later explained as an acronym for the Youth International Party. They planned outdoor concerts, nonviolent self-defense classes, guerrilla theater, and a "nude-in" on a Chicago beach.

In March, representatives of various left-wing and radical student groups met in Lake Villa, Illinois, to discuss coordination of the protests and demonstrations planned for the Democratic convention. Tom Hayden and Rennie Davis drafted a proposal for various protests of the Vietnam War and social injustice, culminating with a mock funeral march to the convention hall on the night Johnson was to be renominated. The Lake Villa proposal advised that "the campaign should not plan violence and disruption against the Democratic National Convention. It should be nonviolent and legal." The National Mobilization Committee sought permits for the proposed march, and the Yippie leaders applied for permits to sleep in the city parks, but in negotiations that continued to the week of the convention, the Daley administration refused almost all permit requests.

Confrontations in Chicago

On the eve of the convention, Mayor Daley, citing intelligence reports of potential violence, put the 12,000 members of the Chicago Police Department on twelve-hour shifts and called for the governor to activate the National Guard. The U.S. Army placed 6,000 troops in position to protect the city during the convention. Both the police and the demonstrators organized workshops for training in the event of violence. The estimated number of demonstrators who came to Chicago during convention week was about 10,000, dramatically less than earlier predictions, but the police were determined to present a show of force and to enforce the 11:00 p.m. curfew in the parks.

Beginning on Sunday, August 25, the police and demonstrators clashed in city parks where many of the protests were staged and where visiting demonstrators hoped to sleep. For three nights, the aggressive police sweep through Lincoln Park was met with the demonstrators' taunting and occasional rocks. With tear gas and clubbings, the police forced demonstrators out of the park and into commercial areas, where demonstrators smashed windows. Police repeatedly targeted journalists and destroyed their cameras.

Violence escalated on the afternoon of August 28, when police at the week's largest rally charged through the crowd in Grant Park to prevent a man from lowering a U.S. flag. Many in the crowd met the police charge with a volley of rocks and improvised missiles. After some measure of peace returned, David Dellinger attempted to negotiate a permit to march to the convention hall. When the city denied the permit and demonstrators attempted to regroup in front of one of the convention delegates' hotels, police lost control of the crowd and violently attempted to clear a street intersection. Television cameras recorded indiscriminate police brutality while demonstrators chanted "The whole world is watching." Inside the convention hall that night, Senator Abraham Ribicoff of Connecticut condemned the "Gestapo tactics on the streets of Chicago," while Mayor Daley, in full view of television cameras, shouted obscenities and anti-Semitic slurs at the senator. Hubert Humphrey won the presidential nomination that night, but the nationally broadcast images of police violence and of Daley's tirade became the lasting memories of the convention.

Investigating the violence

The violence surrounding one of the essential rites of American democracy deepened the widespread perception that the nation faced a political and cultural crisis in 1968. The city of Chicago, the U.S. Department of Justice, the House Committee on Un-American Activities, and the presidentially appointed National Commission on the Causes and Prevention of Violence all responded with investigations of the violence. Within days, the Daley administration issued the first report, blaming the violence on "outside agitators," described as "revolutionaries" who came to Chicago "for the avowed purpose of a hostile confrontation with law enforcement." The chair of the House Un-American Activities subcommittee, Richard Ichord, suspected communist involvement in the demonstrations, but his hearings devolved into a bizarre preview of the conspiracy trial when a shirtless, barefooted Jerry Rubin burst into the hearing room with a bandolier of bullets and a toy gun. In December 1968, the report of the National Commission on the Causes and Prevention of Violence labeled the disturbances in Chicago a "police riot" and presented evidence of "unrestrained and indiscriminate police violence on many occasions." The commission's Walker Report, named after its chair Daniel Walker, acknowledged that demonstrators had provoked the police and responded with violence of their own, but it found that the "vast majority of the demonstrators were intent on expressing by peaceful means their dissent."

On September 9, 1968, three days after release of the Daley report, Chief Judge William J. Campbell of the U.S. District Court for the Northern District of Illinois convened a grand jury to investigate whether the organizers of the demonstrations had violated federal law and whether any police officers had interfered with the civil rights of the protestors. The Department of Justice report, however, found no grounds for prosecution of demonstrators, and Attorney General Ramsey Clark asked the U.S. attorney in Chicago to investigate possible civil rights violations by Chicago police.

Indictment

John Mitchell, the new U.S. Attorney General appointed by President Nixon following his inauguration in January 1969, worked with the U.S. attorney's office in Chicago to strengthen draft indictments of demonstrators, and Department of Justice officials asked U.S. Attorney Thomas Foran, a political ally of Mayor Daley, to remain in office and direct the prosecution. On March 20, 1969, the grand jury indicted eight demonstrators and eight policemen. Seven policemen were charged with assaulting demonstrators and the eighth policeman was charged with perjury.

The indicted demonstrators, soon known as the "Chicago Eight," were charged with conspiring to use interstate commerce with intent to incite a riot. Six of the defendants—David Dellinger, Rennie Davis, Tom Hayden, Abbie Hoffman, Jerry Rubin, and Bobby Seale of the Black Panther Party—were also charged with crossing state lines with the intent to incite a riot. The other two defendants, academics John Froines and Lee Weiner, were charged with teaching demonstrators how to construct incendiary devices that would be used in civil disturbances. If convicted of all charges, each of the defendants faced up to ten years in prison. The case entered the court record as *United States v. Dellinger et al.* These were the first prosecutions under the anti-riot provisions of the Civil Rights Act of 1968.

It was an unlikely group to engage in conspiracy. Dellinger, at 54, had been active in pacifist movements for years before the rise of the student protests of the 1960s. Hayden and Davis were skilled organizers with focused political goals, and they had never been interested in the street theater and cultural radicalism of Hoffman and Rubin. John Froines and Lee Weiner were only marginally involved in the planning for the demonstrations, and their participation during the convention differed little from that of hundreds of others. The unlikeliest conspirator was Bobby Seale, who had never met some of the defendants until they were together in the courtroom and who had appeared in Chicago briefly for a couple of speeches during the convention. Seale was one of the founders of the Black Panther Party, which federal and state prosecutors had recently targeted in numerous prosecutions around the country.

The eight were linked less by common action or common political goals than by a shared radical critique of U.S. government and society. Rennie Davis thought the government "lumped together all the strands of dissent in the sixties," and Tom Hayden concluded that the government had "decided to put radicalism on trial." On the witness stand, Abbie Hoffman dismissed the idea of any conspiracy among the eight defendants, adding, "we couldn't even agree on lunch."

Judge and jury

The randomly assigned judge, Julius Jennings Hoffman, became as much of a symbol as any of the defendants. Judge Hoffman's imperious manner and apparent bias against the defendants inflamed tensions in what would have been a confrontational trial under any circumstances. At 73, Hoffman had been on the federal bench since his appointment by Eisenhower in 1953, and lawyers in Chicago described him as a judge who usually sided with the government attorneys. Judge Hoffman was proud of the efficiency with which he managed cases, and from the first encounters with the defense attorneys, he was determined to show that he would exercise strong control over the case. When four of the attorneys serving the defense during the pretrial proceedings withdrew from the case before the start of the trial, Hoffman held them in contempt, ordered their arrest, and had two of them jailed. A nationwide protest of prominent lawyers convinced Judge Hoffman to relent and accept the new defense team of William Kunstler and Leonard Weinglass. Throughout the trial, Kunstler and Weinglass aggressively challenged Judge Hoffman's procedural rulings, which almost uniformly affirmed the motions of the prosecution.

In his examination of prospective jurors, Hoffman ignored all but one of the questions submitted by the defense attorneys and never asked potential jurors about pretrial publicity or about their attitudes toward student radicals or the Vietnam War. The jury of ten women and two men was selected in a day. Within a week, Hoffman learned that the homes of two jurors had received identical letters saying that the Black Panthers were watching them. After one of those two jurors acknowledged that she could not be impartial in light of the threat, the judge replaced her with an alternate juror and sequestered the remaining jurors for the duration of the trial. Seale denied any Black Panther involvement with the letters.

A mistrial for Bobby Seale

Conflict over the defense attorneys reemerged when Bobby Seale refused to be represented by anyone other than Charles Garry, who originally agreed to represent the defendants but remained in California because of an illness. Judge Hoffman refused Seale's subsequent request to represent himself, and Seale responded with a barrage of courtroom denunciations of the judge as a "pig," a "fascist," and a "racist." When the prosecuting attorney accused Seale of encouraging Black Panthers in the courtroom to defend him, the proceedings degenerated into worse shouting matches. Seale condemned the judge for keeping a picture of the slave owner George Washington above the bench, and Hoffman then followed through on his repeated warning to restrain Seale. In what provided for many the indelible image of the trial, Judge Hoffman ordered U.S. marshals to bind and gag Seale before his appearances in the courtroom. Hoffman allowed Seale in court without restraints the following week, but when Seale argued for his right to cross-examine a witness, Judge Hoffman sentenced him to four years in prison for contempt of court and declared a mistrial in the prosecution of Seale. The Chicago Eight were now the Chicago Seven.

The government's case

Seale's attempts to cross-examine witnesses came as the government presented its case against the defendants. Led by Thomas Foran and Assistant U.S. Attorney Richard Schultz, the government prosecutors relied primarily on the testimony of undercover policemen and informers. Police officer Robert Pierson described how he let his hair grow, rented a motorcycle, and dressed in biker clothes for convention week. He testified that he heard Abbie Hoffman say that the demonstrators would break windows if the police pushed them out of Lincoln Park for a second night, and that Rubin, Seale, and Davis had urged crowds to resist the police or to employ violence. William Frapolly, another policeman, told the court how he enrolled in an Illinois college, grew sideburns and a goatee, and then joined Students for a Democratic Society, the National Mobilization Committee, and other peace groups. Frapolly testified that he had attended various planning meetings and that he had heard nearly all of the defendants state their intention to incite confrontations with the police and to promote other civil disturbances. He also testified that Wiener and Froines had openly discussed the use of incendiary devices and chemical bombs. The government called 53 witnesses, most of whom recounted similar encounters with the defendants.

The defense strategy

The defendants and their attorneys went well beyond the rebuttal of the criminal charges and sought to portray the proceedings as a political trial rather than a criminal prosecution. In their legal arguments, in their courtroom behavior, and in their numerous public appearances, they challenged the legitimacy of the court and the judge as well as the substance of the indictment. The trial became for the defense an opportunity to portray the dissent movement that had converged on Chicago for the Democratic Convention.

The defense called more than 100 witnesses, many of them participants or bystanders in the clashes between the police and the demonstrators. The jury heard repeated testimony about unprovoked police violence and the extensive injuries among the demonstrators. Well-known writers and performers, including Allen Ginsberg, William Styron, Dick Gregory, Norman Mailer, Arlo Guthrie, and Judy Collins, testified to the peaceful intent of the defendants. The judge denied the request to subpoena President Johnson. Mayor Daley appeared as a defense witness but said little as the judge upheld the government's objection to most of the defense questions.

Abbie Hoffman and Rennie Davis were the only defendants to testify. Abbie Hoffman described himself as a resident of the Woodstock Nation and an orphan of America, and he offered a lengthy narrative of his involvement in politics and the origins of the Yippie movement. Davis recounted his role in the organization of the demonstrations and his encounters with the police during the convention. On cross-examination, the government attorneys attempted to establish that use of the words "revolution" and "battle" constituted incitements to riot, but the exchanges with the defendants made clear how difficult it was to connect demonstrators' rhetoric with the violence in Chicago.

Procedural disputes

Much of the trial was consumed by arguments over procedure. Even before the trial started, Judge Hoffman granted only thirty days for pretrial motions rather than the six months requested by the defense. The judge denied the defense attorneys' access to government evidence obtained without a warrant and barred the defense from submitting the Lake Villa document in which Hayden and Davis set out their non-violent strategy. Judge Hoffman prohibited former Attorney General Ramsey Clark from testifying about his opposition to prosecution of demonstrators, and Hoffman sharply limited the defense lawyers' ability to question Mayor Daley. Frequently the trial was interrupted by arguments over seemingly petty questions: Could the defendants distribute birthday cake in the courtroom? Could the defendants use the public restrooms, or should they be limited to the facilities in the holding rooms? Could the musician witnesses sing the songs they performed at demonstrations, or was the judge correct in insisting that they recite lyrics?

Court theater

For the public that followed the trial in the daily media, the substantive arguments and procedural questions were overshadowed by the intentionally subversive behavior of the defendants and the high-handed dramatics of the judge. Jerry Rubin pleaded not guilty with a raised fist. When introduced to the jury, Abbie Hoffman blew them a kiss (and Judge Hoffman ordered them to "disregard that kiss"). The defendants often refused to rise when so instructed. On the day of the Moratorium to End the War in Vietnam, the defendants draped a Viet Cong flag over the defense table. Throughout the trial various defendants called out obscenities and labeled the judge and prosecutors liars or Gestapo officers. In the most theatrical display of contempt for judicial authority, Abbie Hoffman and Jerry Rubin entered the courtroom in judicial robes and then flung them to the floor and stomped on them.

Judge Hoffman was all too easily provoked by the antics of the defendants, and his own instinct for the theatrical added to the carnival atmosphere. By all accounts, his exaggerated reading of the indictment left the jury with no doubt about his opinion of the defendants' guilt. He returned the defendants' name calling and publicly referred to Weinglass as a "wild man." Reporters described his "mimicking" voice as he read the Seale contempt convictions. Judge Hoffman defended himself against personal insults from the defendants, such as when he answered Seale's cry of "racist!" with an account of his pro-civil rights decisions. The defendants believed Judge Hoffman intentionally mispronounced their names, such as when he repeatedly called Dellinger "Dillinger."

Contempt and a verdict

For all the apparent anarchy in courtroom, Judge Hoffman issued no contempt orders until the argument phase closed. Then, while the jury deliberated, the judge cited the defendants and their lawyers for 159 counts of criminal contempt and sentenced them to prison terms ranging from less than three months for Lee Weiner to more than four years for Kunstler. Some of the convictions were for courtroom outbursts and profanities, many were for laughter, and others were based on the refusal of a defendant to rise as the judge entered or left the courtroom. The lawyers' were repeatedly convicted of contempt for persisting in offering motions or challenging a ruling of the judge. The disparities in the sentences surprised many courtroom observers. Abbie Hoffman received a much shorter sentence for the cited instances of sarcasm and personal insults than Tom Hayden received for his challenges to the judge's procedural decisions.

After five days of deliberation, the jury on February 19 acquitted all seven defendants of conspiracy and acquitted Froines and Weiner on all charges. The jury found the five defendants (other than Froines and Weiner) guilty of traveling between states with the intent to incite a riot. Judge Hoffman imposed the maximum sentence of five years in prison on each of the defendants found guilty.

In a separate proceeding in the Northern District of Illinois, a jury acquitted seven of the eight indicted policemen. The case against the eighth was dropped.

Appeals

The defendants and their attorneys appealed to the U.S. Court of Appeals for the Seventh Circuit for a reversal of the criminal convictions and the contempt citations. They argued that the anti-riot provisions of the Civil Rights Act were unconstitutional, that Judge Hoffman's prejudice against the defendants made a fair trial impossible, that they had been denied the right to present a full defense and that they had been denied the right to an impartial jury. They argued that the judge should not have waited until the end of the trial to issue contempt orders and that the conduct cited did not legally constitute contempt. They also argued that the excessive sentences for contempt violated the requirement for a jury trial in any proceeding resulting in greater than six months imprisonment.

On November 21, 1972, an appeals court panel of Judges Thomas E. Fairchild, Wilbur J. Pell, and Walter J. Cummings unanimously overturned the defendants' criminal convictions. The court of appeals found that Judge Hoffman had erred in not asking potential jurors about political and cultural attitudes or about exposure to pretrial publicity, that he had improperly excluded evidence and testimony, and that his failure to notify the defense of his communications with the jury was ground for reversal. In unsparing language, the court of appeals censured Judge Hoffman and the government attorneys for their open hostility toward the defendants and their failure to fulfill "the standards of our system of justice." Their demeanor alone, the court concluded, was sufficient reason to reverse the conviction. The reversal left open the government's option of retrying each of the defendants individually, and the court of appeals reviewed the evidence that it believed a jury might find sufficient for conviction. In January 1973, the U.S. Department of Justice announced that it would not pursue any further prosecution. Only Judge Pell found the Anti-Riot Act to be unconstitutional, so that statute stood.

On May 11, 1972, in a separate proceeding, the same panel of judges on the court of appeals had declared some of the contempt charges against the lawyers to be legally insufficient, and the court reversed all other contempt convictions, which were remanded for retrial before another judge. Judge Edward T. Gignoux, of the U.S. District Court for Maine, was assigned by Chief Justice Warren Burger to preside at the retrial that began in October 1973. The government reduced the number of contempt charges and thereby avoided the requirement of the court of appeals that any defendant subject to more than six months' imprisonment be tried before a jury. Gignoux convicted Dellinger, Hoffman, Rubin, and Kunstler of a total of thirteen contempt charges, but the judge rejected the U.S. attorney's argument that "substantial jail sentences" were necessary to protect the judicial process and deter others of such misbehavior. Gignoux thought that the behavior of the defendants and their lawyers could not be considered "apart from the conduct of the trial judge and prosecutors. Each reacted to provocation by the other, and the tensions generated during four and a half months of so acrimonious a trial cannot be ignored." He was satisfied that the judgment alone preserved the integrity of the trial process.

Legacy

The judicial rebuke of Judge Hoffman prompted only minor notice in the national media that had so closely followed the trial. In many ways the cultural and political moment that defined the trial had passed by the fall of 1972. Even the judges of the U.S. court of appeals felt the need to remind readers of their opinion of how divided the country had been in 1968. The killings at Kent State University in May 1970 had changed forever the youth protest movement, which lost much of its political focus. Left-wing political groups like the Students for a Democratic Society had since splintered, leaving older leaders like Tom Hayden permanently alienated from the increasingly violent agenda of groups like the Weather Underground. The federal government again relied on the Anti-Riot Act to bring charges against anti-war protestors at the Mayday demonstration in 1971, when Abbie Hoffman, John Froines, and Rennie Davis were among those arrested, but the U.S. Court of Appeals for the District of Columbia Circuit blocked most of the prosecutions, and the same court in 1973 found that the mass arrests of nearly 8,000 demonstrators had violated the Fourth Amendment of the Constitution. The Chicago trial had established no precedent for use of the Anti-Riot Act against political demonstrators. The trial of the Chicago Seven lived on less as a legal milestone than as a cultural marker of dissident youth culture in the 1960s and the political divisions surrounding the Vietnam War.

The Judicial Process: A Chronology

September 9, 1968

Grand jury convened in the U.S. District Court for the Northern District of Illinois to investigate whether any demonstrators violated federal law and whether Chicago police officers violated the civil rights of demonstrators.

March 20, 1969

Grand jury in the U.S. District Court for the Northern District of Illinois indicted eight persons on charges of conspiracy to travel in interstate commerce with the intent to incite riots in Chicago. Six of the defendants were indicted on individual charges of traveling in interstate commerce with the intent to incite a riot, in violation of the Anti-Riot Act. On the same day, the grand jury indicted seven Chicago police officers on charges of depriving individuals of their civil rights and an eighth police officer of perjury before the grand jury.

April 9, 1969

Defendants in the conspiracy case were arraigned in the district court and pleaded not guilty.

September 24, 1969

Start of the conspiracy trial.

November 5, 1969

Judge Julius Hoffman declared a mistrial in the prosecution of Bobby Seale and severed his case from the remaining seven defendants. Hoffman also convicted Seale on sixteen counts of contempt and sentenced him to four years in prison.

February 14, 1970

Judge Julius Hoffman convicted the seven defendants and their two attorneys of a total of 159 charges of criminal contempt for behavior throughout the trial.

February 19, 1970

The jury acquitted all defendants of the conspiracy charge and defendants Froines and Wiener of all charges. The jury found the other five defendants guilty of violating the Anti-Riot Act.

May 11, 1972

The U.S. Court of Appeals for the Seventh Circuit reversed most of the contempt convictions, dismissed others, and remanded the remaining contempt charges for retrial by another judge in the district court. On the same day, the U.S. Court of Appeals for the Seventh Circuit, in a separate opinion, dismissed four counts of contempt against Bobby Seale and remanded the remaining twelve contempt specifications against Seale for retrial by another judge.

November 21, 1972

The U.S. Court of Appeals for the Seventh Circuit reversed the convictions of the five defendants on the charge of intent to incite a riot, and the court of appeals remanded the cases to the district court for retrial at the discretion of the government.

January 4, 1973

Attorney General Richard Kleindienst announced that the government would not retry any of the defendants on the charge of intent to incite a riot.

December 6, 1973

Edward Gignoux, sitting by assignment in the District Court for the Northern District of Illinois at the retrial of the contempt charges, dismissed all contempt charges against two of the defendants and attorney Leonard Weinglass, and convicted three of the defendants and attorney William Kunstler of a total of thirteen contempt charges. Gignoux did not impose any further jail sentence.

The Federal Courts and Their Jurisdiction

U.S. District Court for the Northern District of Illinois

The Chicago Eight, later Seven, were indicted in the U.S. District Court for the Northern District of Illinois on charges of conspiracy to incite riots and on individual charges of intent to incite riots or to promote the use of incendiary devices. The court's chief judge, William Campbell, presided over the grand jury investigation. Campbell was randomly selected as the trial judge following the grand jury's indictment, but he recused himself because of his familiarity with the evidence presented to the grand jury. Then Judge Julius Hoffman was randomly selected to preside over the trial.

When the defendants appealed their convictions on criminal contempt, all of the district court's active judges, except for Judge Hoffman, petitioned the U.S. Court of Appeals for the Seventh Circuit for permission to file a brief supporting the broad authority and discretion of a trial judge to punish contempt. The court of appeals denied permission, saying that it would be almost impossible for the district judges to avoid the appearance of supporting one side in the dispute over Judge Hoffman's contempt charges. More than two years later, the U.S. court of appeals reversed the contempt convictions and remanded them for retrial by another judge in the district court. At the request of the chief judge of the court of appeals, Chief Justice Warren Burger designated Judge Edward Gignoux, of the U.S. District Court of Maine, to serve on temporary assignment as the judge of the retrial of the contempt charges. Gignoux presided over the trial that ended on December 6, 1973, with the conviction of three defendants and one of their attorneys on thirteen counts of contempt.

The district courts were established by the Congress in the Judiciary Act of 1789, and they serve as the trial courts in each of the judicial districts of the federal judiciary. The U.S. District Court for the Northern District of Illinois was established in 1855, when Congress divided Illinois into two judicial districts. Illinois was subsequently divided into three judicial districts, but the Northern District has always included Chicago. The court's jurisdiction over the Chicago conspiracy trial was based on federal laws making it a crime to travel across state lines with the intent to incite riots and on laws making it a crime to demonstrate the use or manufacture of explosives that might be used to disrupt commerce.

U.S. Court of Appeals for the Seventh Circuit

The five defendants found guilty in the Chicago conspiracy trial appealed their convictions to the U.S. Court of Appeals for the Seventh Circuit. All seven defendants and their two attorneys also appealed their contempt convictions to the same court.

A panel of three judges, Walter Cummings, Thomas Fairchild, and Wilbur Pell, heard arguments in both appeals. On May 11, 1972, in an opinion written by Judge Cummings, the panel reversed the contempt convictions of all of the defendants and remanded the contempt charges to the district court for retrial. The panel dismissed some of the contempt convictions of attorneys Kunstler and Weinglass and reversed the attorneys' other convictions, which were also remanded to the district court. On November 21, 1972, in an opinion written by Judge Fairchild, the panel reversed the convictions on the charge of violating the Anti-Riot Act and remanded the individual cases to the district court for retrial at the discretion of the government attorneys. By a 2–1 vote, the court upheld the constitutionality of the Anti-Riot Act, and Judge Pell wrote a dissenting opinion explaining why he thought the act was unconstitutional.

The U.S. Court of Appeals for the Seventh Circuit heard various other cases related to the conspiracy trial. In the fall of 1969, the court of appeals upheld a district judge's decision rejecting the National Mobilization Committee's motion for a court order halting the grand jury investigation of the demonstrators and for an order declaring the Anti-Riot Act unconstitutional. In May 1972, the court of appeals dismissed four of Bobby Seale's contempt convictions, reversed the other twelve, and remanded the remaining charges to the district court for retrial before another judge. The court of appeals rejected the appeal of the three defendants and attorney William Kunstler, who had been found guilty of contempt in the retrial conducted by Judge Gignoux. In 1981, following release of information about private communications between Judge Hoffman and the U.S. attorney during the original trial, the court of appeals upheld Judge Gignoux's decision not to reverse the contempt convictions.

The U.S. courts of appeals were established by the Congress in 1891. A court of appeals in each of the regional judicial circuits was established to hear appeals from the federal trial courts, and the decisions of the courts of appeals are final in many categories of cases. The Seventh Circuit consists of Illinois, Indiana, and Wisconsin, and the Seventh Circuit court of appeals has always met in Chicago.

Legal Questions Before the Federal Courts

1. *Were the seven defendants guilty of engaging in a conspiracy to incite a riot?*

No, said the jury in the district court trial.

The indictment described a conspiracy of the eight defendants, eighteen unindicted coconspirators, and other unknown persons, who traveled in interstate commerce with the intent to incite a riot and to commit overt acts to promote and carry out the riot, all in violation of a recent statute passed by Congress in response to the urban riots of the mid-1960s. The defendants were also accused of conspiring to teach the manufacture and use of incendiary devices and to interfere with the official duties of firemen and law enforcement officers. The indictment specified meetings at which various defendants planned the demonstrations and confrontations with law enforcement officers. The indictment also listed speeches and meetings that allegedly constituted the overt acts required for conviction under the Anti-Riot Act.

The government prosecutors argued that the defendants shared a "tacit understanding" of their common goal of provoking a riot, although the eight never met as one group. The defense attorneys described the conspiracy charge as absurd on the face of it, and directed most of their arguments to disproving the charges of intent to incite a riot.

2. *Did the defendants violate the Anti-Riot Act by using interstate commerce with the intent to incite a riot and by committing at least one overt act to promote a riot?*

The jury found five defendants guilty of the charge. The U.S. court of appeals reversed that decision because of errors by the trial judge but found that some of the evidence might be sufficient for conviction if the government chose to retry the five persons in individual trials.

The indictment charged David Dellinger, Rennie Davis, Tom Hayden, Abbie Hoffman, Jerry Rubin, and Bobby Seale with individual violations of the Anti-Riot Act. The indictment specified evidence of intent prior to interstate travel and evidence of overt acts by which each of the six defendants incited a riot during the convention week in Chicago. Seale's case was separated from the others by Judge Hoffman, and the remaining five defendants charged with intent to incite a riot were found guilty by the jury.

The U.S. Court of Appeals for the Seventh Circuit reversed the convictions, but concluded that the evidence presented for each defendant might reasonably be interpreted by a jury as proof of guilt. In their detailed review of the evidence against each defendant, the three judges who heard the appeal found that the evidence of overt acts of inciting a riot was clearer than the evidence of an earlier intent to incite a riot. One of the judges did not find any reasonable evidence of earlier intent in the case of Dellinger. The court of appeals judges did not conclude that any of the defendants was guilty, only that a jury might determine guilt or innocence based on the evidence presented at the original trial.

The court of appeals left for the government the option to retry any or all of the defendants, but the court commented on several issues that were likely to arise in a new trial. The court of appeals dismissed the defendants' claim that the testimony of undercover policemen violated their constitutional rights, and it denied that defendants had a right to address the jury. In a decision that may have convinced the government not to retry, the court of appeals, citing a recent Supreme Court decision, said that in any further proceedings, the defendants had a right to review logs of the government's electronic surveillance of them and a right to a hearing to determine if evidence obtained through that surveillance violated the defendants' constitutional rights.

On January 4, 1973, Attorney General Richard Kleindienst announced that the government would not retry any of the defendants on the charge of intent to incite a riot.

3. Were John Froines and Lee Weiner guilty of instructing demonstrators in the manufacture and use of incendiary devices?

No, the jury found Froines and Weiner not guilty of the charge.

The indictment charged Froines and Weiner with teaching people how to make and use an incendiary device and with the intent to incite civil disorder and to disrupt interstate commerce through the use of such devices. The U.S. attorneys called on undercover policemen for testimony that Froines and Weiner had discussed plans to use flares as weapons, to purchase chemicals for stink bombs, and to make Molotov cocktails for firebombing the parking garage under Grant Park. On cross-examination, the principal government witness admitted that he heard Froines say he didn't know how to make a Molotov cocktail. In their closing arguments, both defense attorneys challenged the credibility of the testimony about the Grant Park garage and emphasized that police never found any physical evidence of firebombs or materials to be used in the manufacture of bombs.

4. Was the Anti-Riot Act of 1968 unconstitutional?

No, the U.S. Court of Appeals for the Seventh Circuit, in a 2–1 decision, decided that the act did not violate the Constitution.

In their appeal, the defendants challenged the constitutionality of the Anti-Riot Act under which they had been convicted. Judges Thomas Fairchild and Walter Cummings found that the act was not so vague or so broad as to be unconstitutional, although they found that the case raised difficult questions. The judges were satisfied that the act required a sufficiently close relationship between speech and action that demonstrated intent to incite a riot. The act's requirement of "an overt act" in support of inciting a riot was enough to prevent the act from suppressing or "chilling" speech protected by the Constitution.

Judge Wilbur Pell dissented from the majority opinion, and wrote that the Anti-Riot Act was an unconstitutional restriction on free speech. Pell, a recent Nixon appointee, found that the act did not distinguish between speech that advocated violence and speech that was directly related to the incitement of violence. The advocacy of "an idea or expression of belief" could not be limited under the Constitution.

In the fall of 1968, lawyers for the National Mobilization Committee had challenged the constitutionality of the Anti-Riot Act in their suit asking for a court order to halt the grand jury inquiry into the demonstrations. On November 1, 1968, Judge Abraham Marovitz of the district court for the Northern District of Illinois dismissed the suit, and the U.S. Court of Appeals for the Seventh Circuit agreed that the challenge to the statute did not raise sufficient constitutional questions.

5. Were the defendants and their attorneys guilty of criminal contempt?

Judge Hoffman convicted the seven defendants and their two attorneys of 157 counts of criminal contempt. The U.S. Court of Appeals for the Seventh Circuit dismissed some of the charges against the attorneys and reversed all other convictions, which the appellate court sent back to the district court for retrial before a different judge. In the new trial, Judge Edward Gignoux found three of the defendants and one of their attorneys guilty of a combined total of thirteen contempts.

The U.S. court of appeals reversed all of the defendants' contempt convictions and remanded them to the district court for retrial. The court of appeals dismissed some of the contempt convictions of attorneys Kunstler and Weinglass because their actions involved legitimate efforts to defend their clients; the remaining attorney convictions were remanded for new trials. The court of appeals also ruled that any defendant subject to more than six months' imprisonment on the contempt charges would be entitled to a trial by jury.

The court of appeals cited recent Supreme Court decisions that restricted a district judge's authority to issue contempt convictions at the conclusion of a trial if the allegedly contemptuous behavior involved personal insults that would likely create bias in the judge. By the time of the hearings on the Chicago Seven appeals, the government attorneys conceded that the defendants' convictions should be retried before another judge in the district court, and the government's decision to drop many of the charges eliminated the need for any jury trials.

Judge Edward Gignoux presided over the retrial of the fifty-two remaining contempt charges. Gignoux quickly dismissed two charges and acquitted the defendants of twenty-four others, including all of those pending against John Froines and Lee Weiner. Following a trial of more than four weeks, Gignoux's decision on the remaining specifications rested on the criteria that the court of appeals had prescribed for determining guilt: the contemptuous behavior must have occurred in the court or close enough to obstruct the proceedings; the conduct must have violated the expected behavior in a courtroom; the individual must have intended to disrupt the court proceedings; and the conduct must have resulted in an obstruction of the courtroom.

Gignoux found David Dellinger guilty of seven contempt charges, most involving repeated insults directed at the judge while the jury was present. Jerry Rubin and Abbie Hoffman were found guilty of two charges each, including their appearance in the courtroom in judicial robes. William Kunstler was guilty of two contempt charges for extended attacks on the judge that resulted in a significant disruption in the courtroom. Gignoux imposed no jail time for any of the contempt convictions.

6. Did the jury selection process protect the defendants' right to a fair trial?

No. The U.S. Court of Appeals for the Seventh Circuit found that the district judge was in error for failing to ask potential jurors about their exposure to pretrial publicity. The court of appeals also found that the district judge should have asked potential jurors about their attitudes toward the Vietnam War, the counterculture, and the Chicago police.

The defendants claimed that the "perfunctory" jury selection, completed in one day, did not solicit the information necessary to make reasoned challenges to jurors. Judge Hoffman asked the defense to submit questions for jurors, but he asked jurors only one question from the defense list. The defense submitted many questions about attitudes toward the Vietnam War, student dissent, and hippie culture. The defense also suggested that the judge ask if the potential jurors knew who Janis Joplin and Jimi Hendrix were, if their daughters wore "brassieres all the time," and if they considered "marihuana habit-forming." The court of appeals considered some of the defense questions "inappropriate," but the court also said that public opinion at the time of the trial was so divided over the Vietnam War and the rise of the counterculture that the judge had an obligation to ask jurors about their views. "We do not believe that a prospective juror is so alert to his own prejudices," that the district court can rely on a general question about the ability to be fair. The defense must be able to ask specific questions about potential prejudices of a juror. The court of appeals decision said that in a case with "widespread publicity about highly dramatic events," the district judge must ask about the impact of pretrial publicity even if, as in this trial, the defense had not raised the issue during the selection of the jury.

The court of appeals did not accept the defendants' other argument that the reliance on voter lists for the selection of grand jury members created a biased grand jury. The court found that the reliance on voter lists underrepresented young people, but that the age imbalance was not so pronounced as to produce a biased grand jury.

7. Did Judge Hoffman unfairly restrict the defense's right to submit evidence and call witnesses?

Yes. The U.S. court of appeals determined that Judge Hoffman had erred in his decision to exclude certain evidence and witnesses for the defense.

The defense attorneys asked to submit various documents as evidence of their claim that the defendants had always intended to engage in peaceful demonstrations at the Democratic National Convention. Judge Hoffman excluded these memos and magazine interviews on the grounds that they were self-serving declarations of the defendants. The court of appeals rejected any blanket rule excluding allegedly self-serving evidence. According to the court of appeals, that standard for evidence was rooted in the long-abandoned rule that defendants in criminal trials could not testify on their own behalf. The court of appeals called special attention to the Lake Villa document drafted by Tom Hayden and Rennie Davis for an organizational meeting in March 1968. It was up to the jury, not the judge, to determine if the Lake Villa policy of nonviolence represented the intentions of the organizers.

The court of appeals also found that Judge Hoffman was wrong to sustain the prosecutors' objection to all expert witnesses called by the defense. The court of appeals supported a trial judge's broad discretion in determining the suitability of witnesses, but Hoffman had been mistaken to exclude the witnesses called to testify about crowd control and law enforcement. The court of appeals determined that these witnesses might have helped the jury assess the defense allegation that police had provoked the violence. The court of appeals upheld Judge Hoffman's decision to exclude expert witnesses who would have testified about racism and social injustice.

The court of appeals found that Judge Hoffman should have allowed former Attorney General Ramsey Clark to testify before the jury. Clark's testimony about a phone call to Mayor Daley in support of permits for the demonstrators would have provided important perspective on the defense claim that the defendants sincerely tried to obtain legal permits.

8. Did the attitude and demeanor of Judge Hoffman and the government attorneys violate the defendants' right to a fair trial?

Yes. The U.S. Court of Appeals of the Seventh Circuit found that the demeanor of the judge and the government attorneys was sufficient reason to reverse the convictions.

The court of appeals found that from the opening of the trial, the district judge made clear his "deprecatory and often antagonistic attitude toward the defense." Judge Hoffman had consistently made sarcastic and gratuitous criticisms of the defense attorneys. The appeals court was especially disturbed that Judge Hoffman had denigrated the defense's key argument that the Daley administration and the Chicago police deliberately provoked the demonstrators. Judge Hoffman's most serious offense, according to the court of appeals, was to make these caustic remarks in front of the jury.

On procedural questions, Judge Hoffman consistently ruled against the defense, and he failed to restrain the U.S. attorney's personal attacks on the defendants. The court of appeals considered U.S. Attorney Thomas Foran's closing arguments, with their emphasis on dress and appearance and references to "evil men" and "violent anarchists," beyond all standards of acceptable behavior. The court of appeals acknowledged the disruptive behavior of the defendants, but that behavior did not justify a disregard of "the high standards for the conduct of judges and prosecutors." "A defendant ought not to be rewarded for success in baiting the judge and the prosecutor."

Legal Arguments in Court

The attorneys for the U.S. government

U.S. Attorney Thomas Foran and Assistant U.S. Attorney Richard Schultz argued that:

1. The seven (originally eight) defendants conspired to provoke government violence against the demonstrators at the Democratic National Convention in Chicago. The prosecutors acknowledged that the defendants had never met as a group, but seven had met in smaller groups to devise their strategy and to coordinate demonstrators' resistance to the police. The testimony of government witnesses established a "tacit understanding" among the defendants and a mutual understanding of the goals of the conspiracy.

2. The defendants intended to incite violence by attracting to Chicago very large crowds to participate in ostensibly peaceful protests of the Vietnam War and social injustice. The defendants incited the demonstrators against the police, the National Guard, and the Army, and the defendants orchestrated confrontations with the intent of provoking law enforcement officers to respond with violence.

3. The defendants privately and in small gatherings, before and during the week of the convention, described their goals of disruption and confrontation, and their goal of inciting not only riots in Chicago, but a popular uprising against the government. The government attorneys cited the defendants' rhetoric about hoping to "smash the city," bringing "the United States military machinery to a halt," and creating the "first steps towards the revolution" as proof that the seven organizers jointly planned to incite violence in Chicago during the Democratic Convention.

4. At least six of the original defendants crossed state lines with the intent to incite violence and thus violated the anti-riot provisions of the Civil Rights Act of 1968.

5. Froines and Weiner discussed the manufacture and possible uses of incendiary devices during the convention.

The attorneys for the defendants

William Kunstler and Leonard Weinglass, attorneys for the seven defendants, rejected a strategy that focused closely on disproving the charges in the indictment. Rather, they emphasized that this was, in their view, more of a political trial than a criminal prosecution. The defense called many witnesses to rebut the testimony of the undercover police, but their goal was always to establish the peaceable intent of the defendants and to expose the political motivation of the prosecution. In their opening and closing arguments, the defense attorneys argued that:

1. The U.S. and Chicago governments engaged in a conspiracy to prevent demonstrations against the Vietnam War and related issues. Kunstler argued that "the police of this city embarked on an organized conspiracy of berserk brutal action against these demonstrators."

2. The prosecution witnesses, who were almost all government employees or informants paid by the government, could not offer impartial or credible testimony. The defense asked the jury to consider why the government had called no bystanders as witnesses of the violence during the convention.

3. The indictment, and particularly the conspiracy charge, was on the face of it absurd. The charges in the indictment implied that seven veterans of the peace movement suddenly rejected their long-standing beliefs and embraced a violent strategy sure to result in their imprisonment.

4. A large number of witnesses, including prominent politicians and entertainers who performed at the protest rallies, testified that they had heard no incitements to violence during the planning and staging of rallies surrounding the convention; nor had they witnessed any diversionary tactics designed to provoke police violence.

5. The indictment represented an assault on First Amendment rights. With their frequent reference to the American Revolution and the Founders, the defense attorneys placed the defendants' activities in Chicago in an American tradition of popular defense of liberties.

Biographies

The judges

Julius Jennings Hoffman (1895–1983)

Presiding judge at the Chicago conspiracy trial

Judge Julius Hoffman earned as much notoriety for his management of the Chicago conspiracy case as the defendants did for their disruptive behavior. Hoffman was born in Chicago and received his law degree from Northwestern University. He entered private practice in Chicago in 1915 and served as general counsel of the Brunswick-Balke-Collender Company (later the Brunswick Corporation) from 1936–1944. Hoffman was elected judge of the Cook County Superior Court in 1947 and was nominated in 1953 by President Eisenhower to the U.S. District Court for the Northern District of Illinois. By the time of the Chicago conspiracy trial, Hoffman was known for his efficient courtroom. Hoffman was randomly assigned to the case after Chief Judge William Campbell recused himself because of his exposure to the evidence presented to the grand jury investigation over which he presided.

Judge Julius J. Hoffman
Courtesy of Bettman/Corbis.

As the trial progressed, Hoffman was unrelenting in his opposition to the defense and in his support for the government attorneys. He rejected the defense motion requesting six months for the preparation of pretrial motions, and he accepted the prosecutions' recommendation of one month; he ordered the arrest of attorneys who assisted in the pre-trial proceedings but who withdrew before the start of the trial; he refused to incorporate all but one of the questions submitted by the defense for prospective jurors; he disregarded Bobby Seale's repeated complaints that he was not being represented by an attorney of his own choice; he rejected crucial evidence of the defendants' intent, and he barred witnesses, like Ramsey Clark, who were prepared to testify to the defendants' intent to abide by the law; he failed to reveal to the defense his communications with the jury as it deliberated; and he delayed issuing any contempt citations until completion of the trial. Many of Judge Hoffman's individual rulings were well within the authority of a district judge, but the cumulative impact, combined with his undisguised disdain for the defendants and their attorneys, set him up for an unusually personal censure from the U.S. Court of Appeals for the Seventh Circuit. That court, in an opinion written by Judge Thomas Fairchild and reversing the criminal convictions, found that "the district judge's deprecatory and often antagonistic attitude toward the defense is evident in the record from the very beginning." Judge Hoffman's order that Seale be bound and gagged brought even greater condemnation from the press and Judge Edward Gignoux, who described the incident as an "appalling spectacle."

Judge Hoffman was not without supporters. On the day after he convicted Bobby Seale of contempt, Judge Hoffman entered the dining room of a private club for his daily lunch and received a standing ovation from the other guests. When the defendants appealed their contempt convictions, Judge Hoffman's colleagues on the district court tried to submit a brief in support of his authority to issue the criminal contempt convictions. During the course of the trial, Judge Hoffman received hundreds of supportive letters from the public. The defendants themselves had mixed feelings about Judge Hoffman, despite their angry, profanity-laden confrontations with him in court, and some later acknowledged that he often made them laugh.

After the close of the trial, Judge Hoffman left for his home in Florida, but he was soon invited by President Nixon to attend the national prayer breakfast at the White House, and the Gridiron Club honored Hoffman at its annual dinner in Washington. He assumed a reduced caseload in 1972, and served on the court until his death. In an interview in 1982, Judge Hoffman said "I did nothing in that trial I am not proud of, I presided with dignity. When I felt I had to be firm, I was firm."

William Joseph Campbell (1905–1988)

Chief judge of the U.S. District Court for the Northern District of Illinois

On September 9, 1968, three days after the Daley administration released its report blaming the violence at the Democratic National Convention on outside agitators, Chief Judge William Campbell of the Northern District of Illinois convened a grand jury to investigate the demonstrators' possible violation of the federal anti-riot law and the police's possible infringement of civil rights. During the convention, Campbell had refused to restrain the police from interfering with reporters. Following release of the Walker Report that attributed much of the violence to the police, Campbell publicly questioned the motivation for release of the report before it was presented to the grand jury, and he suggested that the grand jury might investigate whether the release of the report was an attempt to influence the same grand jury's investigation of the convention violence. After the grand jury indicted eight demonstrators and eight policemen, the court's random assignment procedure originally selected Campbell as the judge for the trial of the eight defendants, but Campbell recused himself because of his detailed knowledge of the evidence presented to the grand jury. As chief judge of the court during the conspiracy trial, Campbell had authority over the rules regulating media access, and he prohibited cameras and sound equipment from public areas of the courthouse.

Campbell was appointed to the U.S. District Court for the Northern District of Illinois by President Franklin Roosevelt in 1940. Campbell was born in Chicago and received his law degree from Loyola

Judge William J. Campbell
Courtesy of the Seventh Circuit Library.

University. He served as U.S. attorney for the Northern District of Illinois for two years before his appointment to the district court. Campbell assumed a reduced caseload in March 1970, but he continued to serve as a senior judge until his death.

Edward T. Gignoux (1916–1988)

U.S. district judge for the District of Maine

Chief Justice Warren Burger assigned Edward Gignoux to be the judge for the retrial of the contempt charges against the defendants and their attorneys. In its reversal of the contempt convictions issued by Judge Hoffman, the U.S. Court of Appeals for the Seventh Circuit cited a recent Supreme Court opinion as authority for requiring a different judge to preside over any retrial of the contempt charges that the government attorneys might choose to pursue. By law, the Chief Justice of the United States may assign a district judge to preside in a district in another judicial circuit if the chief judge of the other circuit specifies a need. (No judge in the Seventh Circuit, which encompasses Illinois, Indiana, and Wisconsin, wanted to preside in the retrial.)

In his personal demeanor and his style of case management, the highly respected Gignoux proved to be the very opposite of Judge Hoffman. Years later, even William Kunstler offered a backhanded compliment. Gignoux, he said, "was a dangerous man. He makes the system look good." Gignoux presided at a trial with no jury because the government attorneys dropped enough contempt charges so that none of the defendants was subject to more than six months' imprisonment if convicted on all counts. Acting Attorney General Robert Bork recommended not retrying the contempts, but the U.S. attorney in Chicago, James Thompson, thought it was important to pursue some of the charges. Gignoux found three of the defendants and attorney William Kunstler guilty of a total of thirteen contempt charges, but Gignoux refused to impose further jail time on any of them. Gignoux's written decision concluded with an eloquent statement on the need for proper courtroom decorum and civility to ensure that citizens can defend their civil liberties.

Judge Edward T. Gignoux

Garbrecht Law Library, University of Maine School of Law.

Gignoux was born in Portland, Maine, and graduated from Harvard College and the Harvard Law School. He was appointed to the U.S. District Court for the District of Maine by President Eisenhower in 1957. Gignoux again served by assignment to another district in 1983 when he presided at the bribery trial of Alcee Hastings, a federal judge in the Southern District of Florida.

Judges of the U.S. Court of Appeals for the Seventh Circuit

Walter Joseph Cummings (1916–1999)

Walter Cummings was appointed to the U.S. Court of Appeals for the Seventh Circuit by President Johnson in 1966, and he served on the court until his death. Cummings was the author of the court's opinion of May 11, 1972, *In re David Dellinger et al.*, which overturned the contempt convictions of the defendants and remanded most of the charges for retrial by a different judge. The opinion ordered that any defendant facing contempt charges subject to more than six months' imprisonment would be entitled to a jury trial. Cummings also authored the court's opinion in *United States v. Bobby G. Seale*, in which the appeals court reversed the contempt convictions of Bobby Seale and remanded for retrial most of those charges, minus four that the court decided were not based on behavior that obstructed the trial.

Judge Walter J. Cummings

Courtesy of the Seventh Circuit Library.

Cummings graduated from Yale University in 1937 and from the Harvard Law School in 1940. He then served as an attorney in the Department of Justice for six years, including a term as assistant solicitor general. He later served as the solicitor general from 1952–1953, the youngest person to hold that position. Before joining the court of appeals, Cummings was in private practice in Chicago for twenty years, during which time he served as president of the Seventh Circuit Bar Association.

Judge Thomas E. Fairchild

Courtesy of the Seventh Circuit Library.

Thomas Edward Fairchild (1912–2007)

Thomas Fairchild was appointed to the U.S. Court of Appeals for the Seventh Circuit by President Johnson in 1966, and he served until his death in 2007, after taking a reduced caseload in 1981. Fairchild wrote the court's opinion of November 1972 in *United States v. David T. Dellinger et al.*, the appeal of the five defendants who had been convicted on the charges of inciting a riot. The court found several grounds for reversal of the convictions, and Fairchild's opinion censured

Judge Julius Hoffman and the government attorneys for their openly critical remarks about the defendants and their attorneys.

Fairchild received his law degree from the University of Wisconsin in 1938, and he worked in private practice before serving as the state attorney general, the U.S. attorney for the Western District of Wisconsin, and as a justice of the Wisconsin Supreme Court. Fairchild was an unsuccessful candidate for the U.S. Senate in 1950 and again in 1952, when he challenged incumbent Senator Joseph McCarthy.

Wilbur Frank Pell, Jr. (1915–2000)

Wilbur Pell was the most recently appointed of the three judges who heard the appeals associated with the Chicago conspiracy trial. Pell had joined the court in April 1970 following his appointment by President Nixon. In a dissent from the majority opinion of the court on the appeal of the convictions on the charge of incitement to riot, in *United States v. David T. Dellinger et al.*, Pell argued that the Anti-Riot Act was an unconstitutional infringement of free speech.

Pell graduated from the Harvard Law School in 1940 and practiced law in his native Indiana for many years. He also served as an FBI agent and as deputy attorney general of Indiana.

Judge Wilbur F. Pell, Jr.
Courtesy of the Seventh Circuit Library.

The defendants

Rennie Davis (1941–)

Rennie Davis, an early member of the Students for a Democratic Society and a veteran organizer, grew up in Virginia, the son of John C. Davis, chairman of President Truman's Council of Economic Advisers. Rennie Davis attended Oberlin College and graduate school at the University of Illinois and the University of Michigan. He joined the SDS and became a close friend of one of its leaders, Tom Hayden. Davis was for several years involved in the group's Economic Research and Action Project, which worked to organize poor urban neighborhoods. By 1967, Davis was increasingly involved in the SDS anti-war activities.

Davis and Hayden joined with the National Mobilization Committee to End the War in Vietnam in planning massive demonstrations to coincide with the Democratic convention in Chicago. Davis met with officials at the Department of Justice to seek their help in obtaining permits from the city of Chicago. He and Hayden also met with attorneys to develop a legal strategy for protection of the demonstrators. In March 1968, Davis and Hayden met with nearly 200 activists and presented the group with an outline of their plans for demonstrations at the convention in Chicago. The document, which Judge Hoffman prohibited the defense from submitting as evidence, stated that the demonstrations "should be nonviolent and legal."

Davis found himself at the center of the police attack on demonstrators in Grant Park on Wednesday of convention week. As he urged the crowd to stay calm, the police moved against the demonstrators and hit Davis on the head. He was both hospitalized and arrested. At the conspiracy trial, Davis was one of only two defendants to testify, and defense attorney Leonard Weinglass asked him to recount the events in Grant Park.

During the months between the defendants' arraignment and the start of the trial, Davis asked Judge Hoffman for permission to travel to North Vietnam and to escort home several American prisoners of war who were released after nego-

Rennie Davis
Courtesy of Bettman/Corbis.

tiations by David Dellinger. Judge Hoffman refused the request, but U.S. Court of Appeals Judge Otto Kerner reversed the ruling, allowing Davis to travel.

Davis was convicted on the charge of intent to incite a riot, but the conviction was reversed by the U.S. Court of Appeals for the Seventh Circuit. The government declined to retry Davis on the Anti-Riot Act charge. Near the close of the trial, Judge Hoffman found Davis guilty of 23 counts of contempt and sentenced him to more than two years in jail. The U.S. court of appeals reversed all of the contempt convictions and remanded them for retrial. The government brought only two of the charges for retrial, and Judge Edward Gignoux found Davis not guilty of the two charges. Gignoux found that Davis's remarks to the jury while Bobby Seale was bound and gagged did not cause the breakdown in courtroom decorum, but rather that the disruption of the trial resulted from "the appalling spectacle of a bound and gagged defendant and the marshals' efforts to subdue him." Gignoux also found that the obstruction of the trial following the revocation of David Dellinger's bail was caused by the behavior of spectators, not the comments of Davis and other defendants.

Davis continued his involvement in anti-war activity, including the Washington, D.C., Mayday actions of 1971, when Davis was among the many arrested for attempting to shut down the federal government. In 1972, Davis went to India to meet the Guru Maharaj Ji, and was converted to the guru's Divine Light Mission. In the 1980s, Davis worked as a venture capital consultant, and in 2008 he is the president of the Foundation for a New Humanity.

David Dellinger (1915–2004)

David Dellinger

Courtesy of Bettman/Corbis.

David Dellinger stood apart from the other defendants in his age and in his lengthy experience as a pacifist and activist for social justice. Dellinger was born in Wakefield, Massachusetts, to a well-connected Republican family. He graduated from Yale University and attended Oxford University. After serving as an ambulance driver for the Loyalists in the Spanish Civil War, he entered Union Theological Seminary to study for the ministry. When Dellinger refused to register for the draft in 1940, he was expelled from the seminary and served one year in a federal prison. When he refused to appear at an draft induction center in 1943, he was again convicted and served two years in a federal prison.

In 1956, Dellinger joined with other Christian pacifists to establish *Liberation* magazine. He organized some of the first protests of American involvement in the Vietnam War. In 1967, as chair of the National Mobilization Committee to End the War in Vietnam, he coordinated a huge anti-war rally in Washington. Dellinger recruited Jerry Rubin to help organize the event that culminated with the march to the Pentagon. Beginning in 1967, Dellinger made several visits to the Paris peace talks, and in the months preceding the conspiracy trial he traveled to Paris to negotiate the release of American prisoners of war and then went to North Vietnam to escort the Americans back to the United States.

Dellinger, as a co-chair of the National Mobilization Committee, was closely involved in planning for the demonstrations in Chicago and hoped to attract huge numbers of people, such as had gathered for the march on the Pentagon in October

1967. At the only rally with a city permit, Dellinger directed the events in Grant Park on Wednesday of convention week, but when police charged on the crowd after a demonstrator lowered the American flag, Dellinger's pleas over the microphone could not stop the violence. Dellinger also clashed with Tom Hayden, who wanted the demonstrators to defend themselves. Later that day, Dellinger attempted to negotiate a permit for a march to the site of the convention, but city officials denied it, and the worst violence of the week followed when police sought to disperse the assembled demonstrators.

Following the indictment of Dellinger and the seven other participants in the demonstrations, he urged the defendants to continue their anti-war activity and to use the trial to publicize their views on the war. Dellinger rejected the advice of potential defense lawyers who suggested their case should focus on narrow legal questions.

The prosecution described Dellinger as "the principal architect especially of the riots which occurred on Wednesday," and the case officially bore his name in the court records. Near the end of the trial, when a police officer serving as a rebuttal witness accused Dellinger of inciting violence in Grant Park, Dellinger responded with what the *New York Times* called a "barnyard epithet," and Judge Hoffman revoked his bail. Dellinger's return to jail prompted the most chaotic scenes in the trial since Bobby Seale had been bound and gagged.

The jury found Dellinger guilty of intent to incite a riot, but the U.S. court of appeals reversed the conviction and remanded the charge for retrial. The government declined to retry him. Near the close of the trial, Judge Hoffman convicted Dellinger of 32 counts of contempt and sentenced him to more than two years and two months in prison. After the court of appeals reversed all of the contempt convictions of the defendants, the government brought eight contempt charges against Dellinger on retrial, and Judge Edward Gignoux found him guilty of seven—the most for any of the defendants or defense attorneys. Dellinger was found guilty on charges related to his courtroom statements, many of them personal insults of the judge. Gignoux found that Dellinger had spoken out when he was adequately represented by his attorneys, and that the outbursts had significantly obstructed the courtroom proceedings. Gignoux did not sentence Dellinger to any additional time in jail.

In 1993, Dellinger published an autobiography, *From Yale to Jail: The Life Story of a Moral Dissenter*.

John Froines

At the time of the trial, John Froines was an assistant professor of chemistry at the University of Oregon. Froines graduated from the University of California at Berkeley in 1963 and received his Ph.D. in chemistry from Yale University in 1966. Froines had known Tom Hayden since they had trained together as community activists. Like his codefendant Weiner, Froines had served as a marshal for the National Mobilization

Committee in Chicago, but Froines and Weiner were the only defendants not related to the leadership of a national organization.

During the defense strategy sessions for the trial, Froines was usually allied with Hayden in support of a clear political focus. Froines traveled with Hayden and Leonard Weinglass to the northern Virginia home of former Attorney General Ramsey Clark to ask him to testify for the defense.

The jury found Froines not guilty of all charges in the indictment, but near the close of the trial Judge Hoffman convicted Froines on ten counts of criminal contempt and sentenced him to six and a half months in jail. The U.S. Court of Appeals reversed the convictions and remanded them for retrial before a different judge in the district court. After the government presented its case in the retrial, the judge acquitted Froines of all remaining contempt charges.

John Froines

Courtesy of Bettman/Corbis.

In the spring of 1971, Froines was arrested and again indicted on charges of violating the Anti-Riot Act following his involvement in the Mayday Tribe effort to shut down the federal government in protest of the war in Vietnam. The government dropped the charge. Froines worked for the Occupational Safety and Health Administration during the Carter administration. He later became a professor of environmental health sciences at the University of California at Los Angeles and, as of 2008, he serves as director of the UCLA Center for Occupational and Environmental Health.

Tom Hayden (1939–)

As a former president of the Students for a Democratic Society and principal author of the key manifesto of student dissent, Tom Hayden was one of the most prominent leaders of the radical political movements that emerged on college campuses in the 1960s. Hayden was born in Detroit, and grew up in Royal Oak, Michigan, where he attended the church of the radio priest and fervent anti-communist, Father Coughlin. Hayden went to the University of Michigan where he served as editor of the *Michigan Daily* and covered the 1960 Democratic convention for his school paper. He joined the Students for a Democratic Society, and as president of the group he drafted the Port Huron Statement that outlined a vision of participatory democracy and personal independence. For several years he worked as a community organizer with an SDS project in Newark, New Jersey. Hayden also became increasingly involved in opposition to American involvement in the Vietnam War. In late 1965, Hayden made his first trip to North Vietnam, and he later returned to that country and Cambodia to secure the release of American prisoners of war.

In the months before the 1968 Democratic National Convention, Hayden and his colleague, Rennie Davis, opened an office in Chicago to plan for a massive demonstration comparable to the anti-war mobilization in Washington, D.C., in October 1967. Although participation in the demonstrations never approached the organizers' goals, Hayden remained as a chief organizer of the week's events, even as the demonstrators seemed to abandon the focused political agenda that Hayden had advocated.

Hayden was one of the six individuals cited by a Daley administration report blaming violence on "outside agitators," and he was one of the eight demonstrators indicted in March 1969. As the defendants planned their strategy, Hayden convinced the defendants to hire Leonard Weinglass, with whom Hayden worked during his community organizing in Newark. Throughout the trial, Hayden was often at odds with other defendants over his determination to maintain a political focus in the trial. Hayden was impatient with what he saw as the unstructured cultural radicalism of Jerry Rubin and Abbie Hoffman.

The jury found Hayden not guilty of the conspiracy charge but guilty of the charge of travel with intent to incite a riot. The conviction was reversed by the

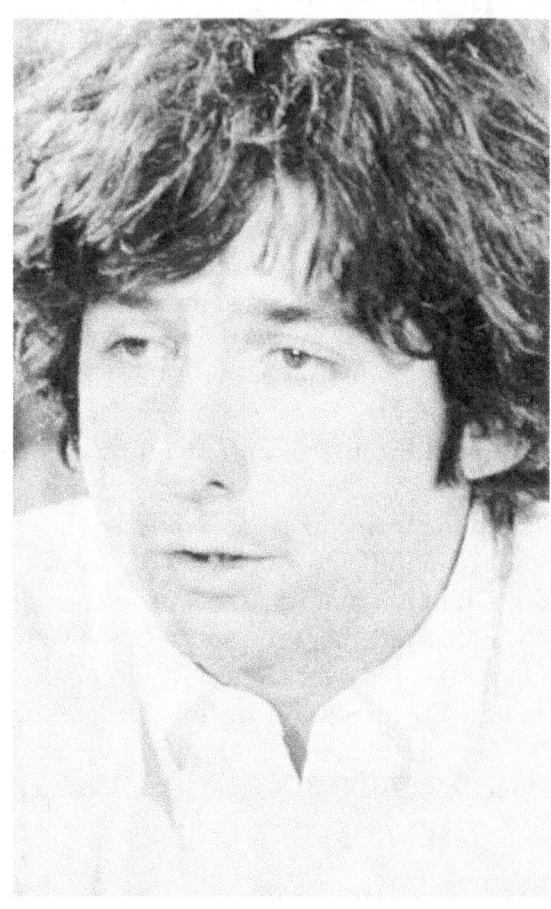

Tom Hayden
Courtesy of Bettman/Corbis.

U.S. Court of Appeals for the Seventh Circuit and remanded to the district court, but the government declined to retry Hayden. Near the close of the trial, Judge Hoffman convicted Hayden on eleven counts of contempt and sentenced him to more than fourteen months in jail. The U.S. Court of Appeals reversed those criminal contempt convictions and remanded the charges for retrial before another judge. The government brought only one of the contempt charges against Hayden on retrial, and Judge Edward Gignoux found Hayden not guilty. Gignoux found that Hayden's statement in court in response to the physical constraint of Bobby Seale was not responsible for the disruption of the courtroom, but rather that the disruption of the trial resulted from "the appalling spectacle of a bound and gagged defendant and the marshals' efforts to subdue him."

Following the Chicago trial, Hayden continued his work in opposition to the Vietnam War. While working with the Indochina Peace Campaign in 1972, he met Jane Fonda, whom he married. Hayden unsuccessfully challenged incumbent U.S. Senator John Tunney in the 1976 California primary. He won election to the California State assembly in 1982 and the California Senate in 1992 and served until 2000.

Abbie Hoffman (1936–1989)

Abbie Hoffman was one of the most visible and familiar of the Chicago Seven defendants, and his style of cultural politics and confrontation defined much of the defendants' response to Judge Julius Hoffman and the government prosecutors. The two Hoffmans engaged in verbal sparring throughout the trial, trading one-liners and gaining much of the attention of the press.

Hoffman was born in Worcester, Massachusetts, and attended Brandeis University and graduate school at the University of California at Berkeley. In the early 1960s, he became increasingly involved in social activism and organized northern support for the civil rights movement in the South. In the mid-1960s, Hoffman moved to New York City and organized political theater. His most famous event was in 1967 at the New York Stock Exchange, where, after notifying the press of their intentions, Hoffman and others entered the visitors' gallery and tossed dollar bills to the trading floor. As Hoffman and other cultural radicals in New York planned political theater to coincide with the Democratic convention in Chicago, they devised the idea of Yippie!, a barely organized movement that would simultaneously mimic and mock a political party. Their plans for

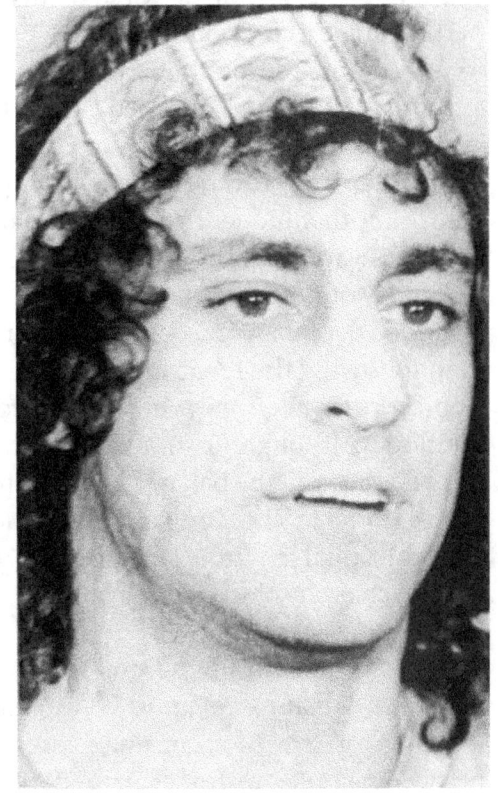

Abbie Hoffman
Courtesy of Bettman/Corbis.

Chicago focused on a Festival of Life, which they envisioned as part music festival and part public presentation of counter-cultural lifestyle, all with the goal of attracting television coverage.

Hoffman and fellow Yippie Jerry Rubin met with the National Mobilization Committee to coordinate demonstrations at the convention, and the Yippie leaders moved to Chicago to negotiate permits for their events in public parks, but the alliance between the cultural radicals and the political organizers was always uneasy.

Hoffman was highly visible in Chicago during most of the convention week, organizing media events and speaking to crowds in Lincoln Park about expected confrontations with the Chicago police. On the night of the worst violence, however, Hoffman was in jail after his arrest for walking around the city with an obscenity written on his forehead in red lipstick. (He claimed he did it to keep his picture out of the newspaper.) Hoffman was among those cited by Mayor Daley's report blaming the violence on outside agitators, and he was one the eight indicted for conspiracy and intent to incite a riot.

Hoffman was one of the two defendants to take the witness stand, and his extended testimony was a tour de force of his absurdist, subversive verbal style. Hoffman's performance in the courtroom was equally notable, seldom missing an opportunity to undermine the legitimacy of the proceedings.

Judge Hoffman convicted Abbie Hoffman on twenty-three counts of criminal contempt but sentenced him to a comparatively light eight months in jail. The U.S. court of appeals reversed the contempt convictions and remanded them for retrial before another judge. The government prosecuted five of the contempt charges, and Judge Edward Gignoux convicted Hoffman on two of the charges and found him not guilty of the other three. Gignoux convicted Hoffman of the charge related to an extended verbal attack, complete with Yiddish insults, delivered against Judge Hoffman following the revocation of David Dellinger's bail and on the charge related to Abbie Hoffman's appearance in the courtroom in judicial robes, which he flung to the floor. Although Gignoux found that the judicial robe episode did not actually impede the trial, the behavior was "so flagrant, so outrageous, and so subversive" that it rose to the level of "an actual obstruction." Gignoux did not sentence Hoffman to any additional jail time. Hoffman's conviction on the charge of intent to incite a riot was reversed by the court of appeals, and the government made no effort to retry him.

Hoffman published several successful books, including *Revolution for the Hell of It* (1968), *Woodstock Nation* (1969), and *Steal This Book* (1970). He went into hiding after an arrest for cocaine possession and lived under an assumed identity for nearly six years. Hoffman surrendered himself in 1980, after his successful work as an environmental organizer made his exposure likely. He was diagnosed with bipolar disorder in 1980, and he committed suicide in 1989.

Jerry Rubin (1938–1994)

Like his fellow Yippie, Abbie Hoffman, Jerry Rubin approached the Chicago conspiracy trial as an opportunity to present a critique of American society and to challenge the legitimacy of the U.S. government.

Jerry Rubin
Courtesy of Bettman/Corbis.

Rubin was born in Cincinnati and attended Oberlin College before graduating from the University of Cincinnati. He worked for a short time as a sports reporter and then enrolled in graduate school at the University of California at Berkeley. He quickly gave up school for political activism and traveled to Cuba. Back in Berkeley, Rubin participated in the Free Speech Movement in 1964. He organized one of the first teach-ins against the Vietnam War. He also developed a reputation for theatrical behavior when, in 1966, he appeared before the House Un-American Activities Committee dressed as an American Revolutionary soldier.

After an unsuccessful run for mayor of Berkeley, Rubin moved to New York where he merged his political activism with an interest in cultural radicalism. He joined with David Dellinger of the National Mobilization Committee to organize a massive protest against the Vietnam War in October 1967, and it was Rubin who proposed to stage the march in front of the Pentagon. With Abbie Hoffman, Rubin was one of the founders of the Yippie movement, and the two of them moved to Chicago in the spring of 1968 to organize Yippie events and to seek city permits for their gatherings in public parks.

In the week before the Democratic convention, Rubin appeared at a rally at the Chicago Civic Center, where he nominated as president a pig, named "Pigasus." (The organizers were arrested and the pig placed in the custody of the local humane society.) Rubin and other Yippies drew on their media skills to spread wild rumors of non-existent Yippie plans, including a supposed effort to put LSD in the Chicago water supply and a plot to place Yippies disguised as bellhops in the hotels serving convention delegates.

The Daley report on the convention demonstrations cited Rubin as one of the "outside agitators" blamed for the violence. While the grand jury investigated possible indictments related to the convention violence, Rubin continued his political theater. When the House Un-American Activities Committee in October 1968 held hearings on the convention violence, Rubin showed up "bearded, beaded, barefooted, and bare-chested," as the *New York Times* described him. At additional HUAC hearings in December, Rubin arrived at the committee room dressed as Santa Claus.

Rubin was convicted of intent to incite a riot, but the U.S. court of appeals reversed the conviction, and the government declined to retry Rubin on the charge.

At the close of the trial, Judge Hoffman convicted Rubin on fifteen charges of contempt and sentenced him to more than two years in jail. The U.S. Court of Appeals for the Seventh Circuit reversed the convictions and remanded the contempt charges for retrial before another judge in the district court. The government prosecuted only three of the contempt charges, and Judge Edward Gignoux convicted Rubin on two of the charges and found Rubin not guilty on the third. The convictions were on charges related to a vocal attack on Judge Hoffman following the revocation of bail for David Dellinger and to Rubin's appearance, along with Abbie Hoffman, in the courtroom in judicial robes, which they flung to the floor.

Rubin drew media attention again in the 1970s when he withdrew from political activity and started work as an entrepreneur. In the 1980s, he joined Abbie Hoffman on a campus tour dubbed the Yippie versus Yuppie debates. Rubin was killed in a pedestrian accident in Los Angeles in 1994.

Bobby Seale (1936–)

Bobby Seale was in many ways the unlikeliest of the conspiracy defendants. Seale had met only one other defendant, Jerry Rubin, before their indictment, and some of the defendants did not meet him until they first appeared in the courtroom. Seale had been in Chicago briefly during convention week to give two speeches. Although his case was severed from the others well before the end of the trial, Seale's confrontations with Judge Hoffman and Hoffman's order to have Seale bound and gagged in the courtroom remain the most powerful examples of the breakdown of the judicial process during the conspiracy trial.

At the time of the Democratic National Convention, Seale lived in Oakland, California, and was chairman of the Black Panther Party. The Black Panthers had not participated in the planning for the Chicago demonstrations, but Seale made an overnight trip to deliver two speeches. Seale spoke to a rally in Lincoln Park and talked of the need for black men to arm themselves in protection against the police, whom he repeatedly referred to as the pigs. In the prosecution's opening statement at the trial, Assistant U.S. Attorney Richard Schultz quoted Seale as saying "if they get in our way, we should kill some of those pigs" and talking about "barbecuing that pork."

The inclusion of Seale in the conspiracy indictment perplexed many people, including the other defendants, but it came at a time of numerous prosecutions of Black Panther Party members in different parts of the country and extensive FBI surveillance of the party members. Shortly before the start of the Chicago conspiracy trial, Seale and other members of the party were indicted in Connecticut on charges of conspiracy to murder a suspected police informant. Because of the indictment, Seale was the only defendant held in jail during the length of his time in the Chicago conspiracy trial.

Seale originally retained the Black Panthers' lawyer Charles Garry as his attorney, and Garry appeared at the defendants' arraignment on April 9. When the trial started in September, Garry was recovering from surgery and could not travel, but Judge Hoffman refused to delay the start of the trial. Seale repeatedly refused to allow William Kunstler to represent him, and

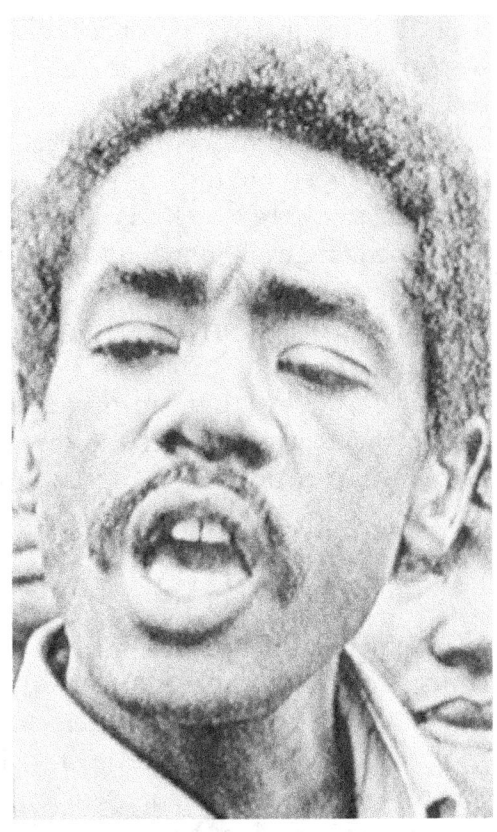

Bobby Seale
Courtesy of Bettman/Corbis.

in a series of increasingly hostile confrontations with the judge, Seale attempted to cross-examine witnesses and otherwise serve as his own counsel. Many of these confrontations ended with Seale's litany of "liar, pig, fascist." On October 29, Judge Hoffman ordered that Seale be bound and gagged by the marshals before any courtroom appearance. Newspapers across the country and television networks carried the courtroom drawings of the violently restrained Seale. Within a week, the judge relented, but when Seale again tried to represent himself, Judge Hoffman on November 5 ordered a mistrial in the prosecution of Seale. Judge Hoffman also convicted Seale on sixteen charges of contempt and sentenced him to four years in prison. The day before, a group of lawyers from across the country filed suit in the U.S. district court asking for an order stopping the trial until Seale was allowed to represent himself, but Judge Edwin Robson dismissed the suit on November 5.

The U.S. Court of Appeals for the Seventh Circuit dismissed four of the contempt convictions of Seale and remanded the other twelve for retrial before another judge in the district court. The government declined to prosecute the contempt charges.

The court of appeals did not rule on Seale's right to a delay in the trial or the right to represent himself, but it found that the trial judge was obligated to investigate Seale's claims that he was not being represented by an attorney of his choice. If such an inquiry had confirmed Seale's account of meetings with his lawyer and found that Seale was "free from ulterior motivation," Judge Hoffman would have been in error to force Seale to rely on Kunstler as his lawyer.

Seale faced trial on the murder conspiracy charges in New Haven, Connecticut, where thousands of protestors, including Abbie Hoffman, criticized the alleged harassment of the Black Panther Party. The jury deadlocked on the charges against Seale, and he never faced a retrial. In 1973, Seale was a candidate for mayor of Oakland, California, but lost to the incumbent in a runoff. Seale later taught political science and served as an assistant to the dean at Temple University in Philadelphia. In 1988, he published a cookbook, *Barbecue'n With Bobby*.

Lee Weiner

Lee Weiner was the least familiar of the defendants, with only limited connections to those who had planned the Chicago demonstrations. At the trial he also was the least visible and, according to Tom Hayden, spent much of his time in court reading the *I Ching*. Weiner was a research assistant in the sociology department at Northwestern University and had served at the Chicago demonstrations as a marshal with the National Mobilization Committee to End the War in Vietnam. He was indicted for conspiracy along with the other seven original defendants, and he and John Froines were indicted on a separate charge of teaching the use of incendiary devices.

Lee Weiner

Courtesy of Bettman/Corbis.

Weiner was acquitted of both the conspiracy charge and the incendiary device charge. Judge Hoffman convicted Weiner on seven charges of criminal contempt and sentenced him to two months and eighteen days in jail. The U.S. court of appeals reversed the convictions and remanded the charges for retrial before another judge. After the government presented its case in the retrial, Judge Edward Gignoux acquitted Weiner of all remaining contempt charges.

Weiner later worked as a political consultant and with the Anti-Defamation League in New York City.

The attorneys

Thomas A. Foran (1924–2000)

U.S. attorney for the Northern District of Illinois

As U.S. attorney for the Northern District of Illinois, Thomas Foran was the lead prosecutor in the Chicago conspiracy trial. Foran, with the assistance of Richard Schultz, presented a case based largely on the testimony of undercover policemen and paid informants, who told of the defendants' plans to disrupt Chicago during the Democratic convention and to provoke law enforcement officers to resort to violence against the demonstrators. Foran aggressively challenged the defense arguments, and his frequent objections were almost always sustained by Judge Hoffman. Throughout the trial, Foran portrayed the defendants as sophisticated revolutionaries who manipulated the alienation of young people. He also emphasized that most of the defendants were much older than the students they attempted to organize. Within days of the close of the trial, Foran continued to stir controversy when he appeared at a public meeting at a Chicago high school and used anti-gay slurs to describe all of the defendants except Bobby Seale.

Thomas A. Foran
Courtesy of Bettman/Corbis.

In its opinion reversing the criminal convictions of five of the defendants, the U.S. Court of Appeals for the Seventh Circuit criticized Foran for his "considerable number" of derogatory comments about the defense. The appeals court found that Foran's final arguments in the case "went at least up to, and probably beyond, the outermost boundary of permissible inferences from the evidence in his characterizations of defendants." The court cited as particularly offensive Foran's references to "evil men" and "anarchists."

The Chicago-born Foran attended Loyola University and the law school of the University of Detroit before entering into private practice in Chicago. He was well connected in Democratic circles in Chicago and was appointed U.S. attorney by President Johnson in 1968. In his short tenure as U.S. attorney, Foran successfully prosecuted a number of individuals involved in organized crime. Following the election of a Republican President, Foran intended to resign on July 1, 1969, but the Nixon administration's Justice Department requested that Foran stay on as U.S. attorney to prosecute the Chicago conspiracy trial. Following his resignation as U.S. attorney in 1970, Foran returned to private practice in Chicago.

William Kunstler (1919–1995)

Attorney for the defendants

William Kunstler served as the lead attorney for the defendants in the Chicago conspiracy trial and cemented his reputation as a lawyer for left-leaning celebrities. Kunstler was born in New York City and attended Yale University. He then served in the military and graduated from Columbia Law School. As a law student he wrote for various publications and read movie scripts for a major studio. In the early years of his law practice in New York, Kunstler also wrote radio scripts. He gained national attention in 1961 with the publication of a book on the controversial death penalty case of Caryl Chessman. Kunstler represented various civil rights leaders in the 1960s, and he also represented celebrity clients like the comedian Lenny Bruce. He agreed to represent Lee Harvey Oswald after the assassination of President Kennedy, and Kunstler later represented Jack Ruby in an appeal of Ruby's conviction for murdering Oswald.

William Kunstler
Courtesy of Bettman/Corbis.

Although Kunstler often left the more detailed legal work of the Chicago trial to his colleague Leonard Weinglass, it was Kunstler who emphasized what he thought was the political character of the trial. He frequently linked the defendants with American Revolutionaries and historical advocates of social justice and political liberty. The trial, according to Kunstler's opening statement, was "a classic example of the Government against the people." "The real conspiracy in this case is the conspiracy to curtail and prevent the demonstrations against the war in Vietnam." Kunstler was also a highly visible advocate for the defendants outside the courtroom.

At the Chicago trial, Kunstler took the lead in challenging Judge Hoffman and the government prosecutors. His confrontations with the judge resulted in Judge Hoffman issuing contempt convictions on thirty-four charges against Kunstler and imposing a jail sentence of more than four years. The U.S. Court of Appeals for the Seventh Circuit dismissed nine of the charges and remanded the rest for retrial before another judge. The government dropped all but six of the charges, and at the retrial, Judge Edward Gignoux found Kunstler not guilty of four of the charges. The first of Kunstler's contempt convictions resulted from an extended diatribe against Judge Hoffman that constituted "outrageous behavior," according to Gignoux, and that resulted in a substantive delay in the trial. The other conviction was based on Kunstler's refusal to obey the judge's order not to discuss a motion in front of the jury. In both instances, Gignoux found that Kunstler's behavior exceeded any definition of "vigorous advocacy" of the defendants' interests. Gignoux imposed no jail sentence on Kunstler or the other defendants convicted of contempt.

In the years following the Chicago conspiracy trial, Kunstler often represented well-known radicals and notorious criminal defendants. He also appeared in movies and television, occasionally playing himself.

Leonard Weinglass (1933–)

Attorney for the defendants

Leonard Weinglass was the younger and less well-known attorney for the defense. Weinglass graduated from George Washington University and the Yale Law School. After service in the Air Force, he practiced law in Newark, N.J., and taught at the Rutgers Law School. He joined the defense for the Chicago case at the request of Tom Hayden, whom he had defended on several minor offenses arising from Hayden's work with the Students for a Democratic Society. Weinglass took responsibility for the defense of Hayden, Rennie Davis, Abbie Hoffman, and John Froines. Weeks before the trial started, Abbie Hoffman invited Weinglass to accompany him to the Woodstock music festival. The defendants later remembered him as the one who "always did his homework and was there with the necessary cases and precedents when they were needed."

Near the close of the trial, Judge Julius Hoffman convicted Leonard Weinglass of fourteen counts of criminal contempt. The U.S. Court of Appeals for the Seventh Circuit dismissed seven of those counts and remanded the others for retrial before another judge. The government attorneys chose to bring only one of the remaining contempt charges against Weinglass in the retrial, and Judge Edward Gignoux found Weinglass not guilty because the alleged contempt had not obstructed the trial nor had it involved personal insults against Judge Hoffman.

Weinglass later reminisced that he had a "sort of wistful regard" for his experience with Judge Hoffman. "He had a razor-like wit which he would use against you in court. I'd find myself angry and upset but amused at the same time."

Leonard Weinglass

Courtesy of Bettman/Corbis.

Weinglass continued to represent leftist clients, including members of the Weather Underground, and controversial criminal defendants.

Richard J. Daley (1902–1976)

Mayor of Chicago

By 1968, Richard J. Daley had been mayor for more than twenty years, and for much of the nation he was the very image of modern Chicago. After service in the Illinois legislature and state government under Governor Adlai Stevenson, Daley became chair of the Cook County Democratic Central Committee in 1953 and was elected mayor two years later. As mayor and party leader, he commanded an extensive organization that ensured his reelection and helped him efficiently deliver municipal services. Daley also promoted investments in major public works and private construction that helped maintain Chicago's status among American cities. His political influence made him an important player in national Democratic politics. By the time of the Democratic convention, however, Daley's style of urban leadership was an anachronism and subject to charges of cronyism and machine politics.

Daley's reputation suffered a serious blow in the spring of 1968 during the riots that followed the assassination of Martin Luther King. The mayor asked the police superintendent to order police to shoot to kill any arsonist and to shoot to maim looters. A national outcry followed. In 1968, Daley's administration was determined to prevent any kind of civil disturbance during the Democratic convention, and officials refused to issue permits requested by demonstrators. The mayor's administration also mobilized an overwhelming force of police and National Guard troops to maintain order in the city.

Mayor Richard J. Daley on the floor of the Democratic National Convention

Associated Press, 1968.

National media covering the convention criticized the police response to the demonstrators, and the television networks broadcast Daley's remarkable tantrum on the floor of the convention. Daley responded to the public criticism with a hastily prepared report that blamed the convention violence on "outside agitators" and a "hard core of revolutionaries."

In January 1970, Mayor Daley appeared as a witness for the defense, but his testimony did little to support the defense argument. Daley insisted he had not ordered the denial of permits for demonstrators, but for the most part Daley offered little beyond praise for his staff and U.S. Attorney Foran. Judge Hoffman sustained most of the prosecution's objections to the defense line of questioning of Daley. Defense attorney Kunstler read into the record an "offer of proof," which allows an attorney to present, away from the presence of the jury, information that the judge had not allowed them to present through examination of a witness. Kunstler's order of proof alleged a conspiracy of Daley and President Johnson, with the cooperation of the U.S. attorney, to prevent any demonstrations against the Vietnam War and social injustice.

Despite the damage to his national reputation following the events of 1968, Daley remained popular in much of Chicago and won reelection to a sixth term in 1975.

Media Coverage and Public Debates

During the Democratic National Convention of August 1968, network television coverage of the confrontations between demonstrators and Chicago police shocked the nation and prompted investigations by the city of Chicago, the House Committee on Un-American Activities, and the President's National Commission on the Causes and Prevention of Violence. The media images of the violence disrupting the political process also intensified demands for the criminal prosecution of the police and the demonstrators. The subsequent trial of the demonstrators, closely followed by the media, became the center of a national debate on the fairness of the federal judicial system and on the culture of dissent that arose in the 1960s.

Media coverage had been central to the debate over the demonstrations surrounding the convention, and it would be a subject of controversy leading up to and throughout the Chicago Seven trial. On the first anniversary of the convention riots and weeks before the opening of the trial, Tom Wicker wrote in the *New York Times* "The miracle of television made it visible to all—pierced, at last, the isolation of one America from the other, exposed to each the power it faced."

Chicago police marshal against demonstrators during the
Democratic National Convention, 1968

Courtesy of the Chicago History Museum.

The role of the media in the Chicago violence was a polarizing issue. In the days following the convention, Mayor Daley demanded prime time on each of the television networks for a response to what he characterized as distorted coverage of the police violence. Several months later, the Walker Report's review of police violence concluded that "newsmen and photographers were singled out for assault, and their equipment deliberately damaged." Shortly after the report was published, U.S. Attorney Thomas Foran alleged that the television networks had staged shots of the demonstrators' injuries at the hands of the police.

As the trial began in September 1969, the district court for the Northern District of Illinois attempted to manage the expected media crush. Chief Judge William Campbell prohibited cameras and sound equipment from all but one room of the courthouse, and Judge Richard Austin dismissed a suit by the American Civil Liberties Union challenging the ban. Austin announced that "the quickest way to end demonstrations is to have all cameras five blocks from the building." Campbell denied a request from over 100 attorneys to move the trial to a larger courtroom that could accommodate more of the press and hopeful spectators who lined up daily outside the federal courthouse, and the U.S. court of appeals upheld Campbell's decision. Judge Hoffman set aside a section of the courtroom for the press with credentials, but he prohibited them from wearing press credentials in the courtroom, explaining that he didn't want his courtroom to look like "a furniture convention." The limited access did nothing to deter press interest in the trial, and around twenty news outlets, including newspapers like the *New York Times* and the *Washington Post,* assigned reporters to cover the full length of the proceedings.

Everyone in the courtroom took notice of the daily coverage of the trial by national print and broadcast media. The defendants' antics and the long list of celebrity witnesses guaranteed an audience well beyond the judge and jury. The defense held daily press conferences during the lunch break until the judge warned them not to comment on the trial in public. Judge Hoffman proved to be equally adept at attracting press comment, and the chief judge of the court later acknowledged that Judge Hoffman "loved the publicity, bad as it was."

The defendants cultivated media coverage outside of the courtroom in their efforts to convince the public that the court proceedings amounted to a political rather than a criminal trial. At night defendants spoke to community meetings and attended fundraisers held by wealthy supporters. One weekend, the defendants traveled to Washington to join a half-million people at a rally against the Vietnam War. Their public appearances could have a less serious side as well. On a visit to Chicago's Second City comedy club, Abbie Hoffman responded to an audience request with a 45-minute satire of Judge Hoffman. In December 1969, the defendants posed in a group photo for a holiday card that urged recipients to "Make a New Year's Resolution—Join the Conspiracy."

Demonstrators during the Democratic National Convention, 1968

Courtesy of the Chicago History Museum.

Washington Post writer Nicholas Van Hoffman noted within the first weeks of the trial that the proceedings had none of the expected characteristics of a criminal trial. "No one here at the Great Conspiracy Trial thinks of its outcome in terms of guilt or innocence. You are for the government or for the defendants." A *Chicago Sun-Times* reporter found the trial "more sideshow than criminal proceeding."

Outside the courtroom, the cultural and political clashes of convention week played on as background for the trial. A series of protests and demonstrations, most of them small and many barely related to the trial, appeared outside the courthouse. The violence of convention week threatened to reappear in October 1969 during the self-styled "Days of Rage" organized by the Weatherman group and other radical groups emerging from the break up of the Students for a Democratic Society. Protestors clashed with Chicago police and smashed store windows, at one point attempting to reach the hotel where Judge Hoffman and his wife lived.

Very different groups of protestors approached the court to protect defendants' right to representation. When Judge Hoffman threatened to hold the pretrial team of defense lawyers in contempt, nationally prominent lawyers and law professors, including future federal judges, converged on the courthouse to demand a mistrial.

The gagging of Bobby Seale, Judge Hoffman's consistently pro-government rulings, and the ill-defined requirements for conviction on the conspiracy charge led many in the press to question the impartiality of the judicial system. Tom Wicker of the

Courtroom drawing of Bobby Seale, seated, bound and gagged during the Chicago conspiracy trial

Howard Brodie, artist. 1969. Library of Congress,
Prints and Photographs Division [LC-USZC4-4870].

New York Times asked if the burden of proof "any longer means anything." J. Anthony Lukas noted the many observers "who view what they regard as the excesses on both sides as damaging to the American judicial process and raising questions as to how a court can effectively dispense justice in cases which arouse such strong political passions." The defendants were only too willing to foster these doubts about justice in the federal courts. Rennie Davis said that "Judge Hoffman presides in every court in this country." Alternatively, the letters to the editors of Chicago newspapers indicated popular support for Judge Hoffman.

The guilty verdict for five of the defendants brought familiar popular protests, including a crowd of 5,000 outside the Chicago courthouse and another demonstration in Washington, D.C., where more than 100 people were arrested. The several appeals that brought reversals of the convictions and a rebuke of Judge Hoffman were prominently reported by the national press, but the popular interest in the case never again rose to the levels seen during the trial phase. The proceedings in the court of appeals had none of the dramatic interest of the trial, and, perhaps more important, the protest movement evident at the Democratic convention declined following the killings at Kent State University in the spring of 1970.

Historical Documents

Testimony of Abbie Hoffman, December 23 & 29, 1969

Abbie Hoffman and Rennie Davis were the only defendants to testify at the trial. Hoffman's appearance was meant to establish the nonviolent intent of the demonstrations and events planned by the Yippies. His opening remarks were more in the nature of a performance than testimony, as was typical of so much of Hoffman's interaction with the court. His answers to the standard opening questions challenged the very forms of a trial and replaced them with something closer to a comedy routine. His claim that he was a resident of Woodstock Nation referred to the book Hoffman published after attending the music festival in August 1969. Hoffman escorted Leonard Weinglass to Woodstock as an introduction to the counterculture. The remarks of December 29 are devoted to the founding and goals of the Yippie party.

    [Document Source: *The Conspiracy Trial*, eds., Judy Clavir and John Spitzer (Indianapolis, IN: Bobbs-Merrill Co., 1970), 344–45, 349–50.]

December 23, 1969

Mr. Weinglass: Will you please identify yourself for the record?

The Witness: My name is Abbie. I am an orphan of America.

Mr. Schultz: Your Honor, may the record show it is the defendant Hoffman who has taken the stand?

The Court: Oh, yes. It may so indicate.

The Witness: Well, it is not really my last name.

Mr. Weinglass: Abbie, what is your last name?

The Witness: Well, there is some confusion about it because, well, my grandfather, he was a Russian Jew, and he decided to protest the anti-Semitism in the Russian Army and he slew—

Mr. Schultz: Objection. If the defendant has a last name, let him state it, but not—

The Court: All we want to know, sir, is your last name.

The Witness: My slave name is Hoffman. My real name is Shaboysnakoff. I can't spell it.

The Court: There is a lawyer who has filed his appearance in the name of Abbie Hoffman for you. You gave him your name as Abbie Hoffman, did you not?

The Witness: Well, no. It was the Government's idea and the name was Abbott Howard.

Mr. Weinglass: Where do you reside?

The Witness: I live in Woodstock Nation.

Mr. Weinglass: Will you tell the Court and jury where it is?

The Witness: Yes. It is a nation of alienated young people. We carry it around with us as a state of mind in the same way as the Sioux Indians carried the Sioux nation around with them. It is a nation dedicated to cooperation versus competition, to the idea that people should have better means of exchange than property or money, that there should be some other basis for human interaction. It is a nation dedicated to—

The Court: Just where it is, that is all.

The Witness: It is in my mind and in the minds of my brothers and sisters. It does not consist of property or material but, rather, of ideas and certain values. We believe in a society—

The Court: No, we want the place of residence, if he has one, place of doing business, if you have a business. Nothing about philosophy or India, sir. Just where you live, if you have a place to live. Now you said Woodstock. In what state is Woodstock?

The Witness: It is in the state of mind, in the mind of myself and my brothers and sisters. It is a conspiracy. Presently, the nation is held captive, in the penitentiaries of the institutions of a decaying system.

Mr. Weinglass: Can you tell the Court and jury your present age?

The Witness: My age is 33. I am a child of the 60s.

Mr. Weinglass: When were you born?

The Witness: Psychologically, 1960.

Mr. Schultz: Objection, if the Court please. I move to strike the answer.

Mr. Weinglass: What is the actual date of your birth?

The Witness: November 30, 1936.

Mr. Weinglass: Between the date of your birth, November 30, 1936, and May 1, 1960, what if anything occurred in your life?

The Witness: Nothing. I believe it is called an American education.

Mr. Schultz: Objection.

The Court: I sustain the objection.

The Witness: Huh.

Mr. Weinglass: Abbie, could you tell the Court and jury—

Mr. Schultz: His name isn't Abbie. I object to this informality.

Mr. Weinglass: Can you tell the Court and jury what is your present occupation?

The Witness: I am a cultural revolutionary. Well, I am really a defendant—full-time.

Mr. Weinglass: What do you mean by the phrase "cultural revolutionary"?

The Witness: Well, I suppose it is a person who tries to shape and participate in the values, and the mores, the customs and the style of living of new people who eventually become inhabitants of a new nation and a new society through art and poetry, theater, and music.

Mr. Weinglass: What have you done yourself to participate in that revolution?

The Witness: Well, I have been a rock and roll singer. I am a reporter with the Liberation News Service. I am a poet. I am a film maker. I made a movie called "Yippies Tour Chicago or How I Spent My Summer Vacation." Currently, I am negotiating with United Artists and MGM to do a movie in Hollywood.

I have written an extensive pamphlet on how to live free in the city of New York.

I have written two books, one called *Revolution for The Hell of It* under the pseudonym Free, and one called, *Woodstock Nation.*

Mr. Weinglass: Taking you back to the spring of 1960, approximately May 1, 1960, will you tell the Court and jury where you were?

Mr. Schultz: 1960?

The Witness: That's right.

Mr. Schultz: Objection.

The Court: I sustain the objection.

Mr. Weinglass: Your Honor, that date has great relevance to the trial. May 1, 1960, was this witness' first public demonstration. I am going to bring him down through Chicago.

The Court: Not in my presence, you are not going to bring him down. I sustain the objection to the question.

The Witness: My background has nothing to do with my state of mind?

The Court: Will you remain quiet while I am making a ruling? I know you have no respect for me.

Mr. Kunstler: Your Honor, that is totally unwarranted. I think your remarks call for a motion for a mistrial.

The Court: And your motion calls for a denial of the motion. Mr. Weinglass, continue with your examination.

Mr. Kunstler: You denied my motion? I hadn't even started to argue it.

The Court: I don't need any argument on that one. The witness turned his back on me while he was on the witness stand.

The Witness: I was just looking at the pictures of the longhairs up on the wall. . . .

The Witness: Yes.

We talked about the possibility of having demonstrations at the Democratic Convention in Chicago, Illinois, that was going to be occurring that August. I am not sure that we knew at that point that it was in Chicago. Wherever it was, we were planning on going.

Jerry Rubin, I believe, said that it would be a good idea to call it the Festival of Life in contrast to the Convention of Death, and to have it in some kind of public area, like a park or something, in Chicago.

One thing that I was very particular about was that we didn't have any concept of leadership involved. There was a feeling of young people that they didn't want to listen to leaders. We had to create a kind of situation in which people would be allowed to participate and become in a real sense their own leaders.

I think it was then after this that Paul Krassner said the word "YIPPIE," and we felt that that expressed in a kind of slogan and advertising sense the spirit that we wanted to put forth in Chicago, and we adopted that as our password, really.

December 29, 1969

The Witness: Anita [Hoffman] said that "Yippie" would be understood by our generation, that straight newspapers like the *New York Times* and the U.S. Government and the courts and everything wouldn't take it seriously unless it had a formal name, so she came up with the name: "Youth International Party." She said we could play a lot of jokes on the concept of "party" because everybody would think that we were this huge international conspiracy, but that in actuality we were a party that you had fun at.

Nancy [Kursham] said that fun was an integral ingredient, that people in America, because they were being programmed like IBM cards, weren't having enough fun in life and that if you watched television, the only people that you saw having any fun were people who were buying lousy junk on television commercials, and that this would be a whole new attitude because you would see people, young people, having fun while they were protesting the system, and that young people all around this country and around the world would be turned on for that kind of an attitude.

I said that fun was very important, too, that it was a direct rebuttal of the kind of ethics and morals that were being put forth in the country to keep people working in a rat race which didn't make any sense because in a few years that machines would do all the work anyway, that there was a whole system of values that people were taught to postpone their pleasure, to put all their money in the bank, to buy life insurance, a whole bunch of things that didn't make any sense to our generation at all, and that fun actually was becoming quite subversive.

Jerry said that because of our action at the Stock Exchange in throwing out the money, that within a few weeks the Wall Street brokers there had totally enclosed the whole stock exchange in bulletproof, shatterproof glass, that cost something like $20,000 because they were afraid we'd come back and throw money out again.

He said that for hundreds of years political cartoonists had always pictured corrupt politicians in the guise of a pig, and he said that it would be great theater if we ran a pig for President, and we all took that on as like a great idea and that's more or less—that was the founding.

Mr. Weinglass: The document that is before you, D-222 for identification, what is that document?

The Witness: It was our initial call to people to describe what Yippie was about and why we were coming to Chicago.

Mr. Weinglass: Now, Abbie, could you read the entire document to the jury.

The Witness: It says:

"A STATEMENT FROM YIP!

"Join us in Chicago in August for an international festival of youth, music, and theater. Rise up and abandon the creeping meatball! Come all you rebels, youth spirits, rock minstrels, truth-seekers, peacock-freaks, poets, barricade-jumpers, dancers, lovers and artists!

"It is summer. It is the last week in August, and the NATIONAL DEATH PARTY meets to bless Lyndon Johnson. We are there! There are 50,000 of us dancing in the streets, throbbing with amplifiers and harmony. We are making love in the parks. We are reading, singing, laughing, printing newspapers, groping, and making a mock convention, and celebrating the birth of FREE AMERICA in our own time.

"Everything will be free. Bring blankets, tents, draft-cards, body-paint, Mr. Leary's Cow, food to share, music, eager skin, and happiness. The threats of LBJ, Mayor Daley, and J. Edgar Freako will not stop us. We are coming! We are coming from all over the world!

"The life of the American spirit is being torn asunder by the forces of violence, decay, and the napalm-cancer fiend. We demand the Politics of Ecstasy! We are the delicate spores of the new fierceness that will change America. We will create our own reality, we are Free America! And we will not accept the false theater of the Death Convention.

"We will be in Chicago. Begin preparations now! Chicago is yours! Do it!"

"Do it!" was a slogan like "Yippie." We use that a lot and it meant that each person that came should take on the responsibility for being his own leader—that we should, in fact, have a leaderless society.

We shortly thereafter opened an office and people worked in the office on what we call movement salaries, subsistence, thirty dollars a week. We had what the straight world would call a staff and an office although we called it an energy center and regarded ourselves as a tribe or a family.

Testimony of Rennie Davis, January 24, 1970

Rennie Davis offered the court his account of the events in Grant Park on the after-noon of August 28. The rally was one of the only events for which the city of Chicago granted a permit, but the event ended with some of the worst violence of the week and heightened tensions leading to an even more violent confrontation that evening in front of one of the conventions' delegates' hotels. Davis testified that he attempted to calm the demonstrators and reduce the risk of police violence in the moments before he was beaten.

[Document Source: *The Conspiracy Trial*, eds., Judy Clavir and John Spitzer (Indianapolis, IN: Bobbs-Merrill Co., 1970), 480–81.]

———————————

Mr. Weinglass: Now, directing your attention to approximately 2:30 in the afternoon of that same day, do you recall where you were at that time?

The Witness: Yes, I was in Grant Park just south of the refreshment stand. I saw a commotion near the flagpole and shortly after that I heard Dave Dellinger's voice. It was clear that something was happening and Dave indicated that he wanted marshals to move to the flagpole, so I then said to everyone there that we should go toward the flagpole.

Mr. Weinglass: When you went to the flagpole, did you have anything in your hands?

The Witness: I had a speaker system with a microphone.

Mr. Weinglass: As you arrived in the vicinity of the flagpole, what was occurring?

The Witness: The flag had been lowered to halfmast and the police were dragging a young man out of the area. The police seemed to be withdrawing from the area as I arrived, and a lot of people who were gathered around the flagpole began to throw anything they could get their hands on at the police who were withdrawing from the crowd. They threw rocks and boards and lunches and anything that was available right on the ground.

Mr. Weinglass: What were you saying, if anything, at that time on the micro-phone?

The Witness: I kept directing the marshals to form a line, link arms, and then I constantly urged the people in the crowd to stop throwing things. I said, "You're throwing things at our own people. Move back."

As our marshal line grew, I urged our marshal line to now begin to move back and move the demonstrators away from the police.

Mr. Weinglass: Where did you go?

The Witness: I continued to stand in front of the marshal line that had been formed.

Mr. Weinglass: What did you then observe happen?

The Witness: Well, at that time another squadron of policemen in formation began to advance towards my position.

I was standing in front of our marshal line sort of sandwiched in between our marshal line and the advancing police formation.

Mr. Weinglass: What were you doing as the police were advancing?

The Witness: Well, as the police advanced, I continued to have my back to the police line, basically concerned that the marshal line not break or move. Then the police formation broke and began to run, and at that time I heard several of the men in the line yell, quite distinctly, "Kill Davis! Kill Davis!" and they were screaming that and the police moved on top of me, and I was trapped between my own marshal line and advancing police line.

The first thing that occurred to me was a very powerful blow to the head that drove me face first down into the dirt, and then, as I attempted to crawl on my hands and knees, the policemen continued to yell, "Kill Davis! Kill Davis!" and continued to strike me across the ear and the neck and the back.

I guess I must have been hit thirty or forty times in the back and I crawled for maybe—I don't know how many feet, ten feet maybe, and I came to a chain fence and somehow I managed to crawl either under or through that fence, and a police fell over the fence, trying to get me, and another police hit the fence with his nightstick, but I had about a second or two in which I could stand and I leaped over a bench and over some people and into the park, and then I proceeded to walk toward the center of the park.

Mr. Weinglass: As you walked toward the center of the park, what, if anything, happened?

The Witness: Well, I guess the first thing that I was conscious of, I looked down, and my tie was just solid blood, and I realized that my shirt was just becoming blood, and someone took my arm and took me to the east side of the Bandshell, and I laid down, and there was a white coat who was bent over me. I remember hearing the voice of Carl Oglesby. Carl said, "In order to survive in this country, we have to fight," and then—then I lost consciousness.

Assistant U.S. Attorney Richard Schultz, closing argument for the government, February 11, 1970

According to Richard Schultz, the seven defendants were united in their determination to provoke violence in Chicago during the Democratic convention. Throughout the trial, the prosecution had attempted to explain how the occasional cooperation of seven individuals constituted a conspiracy. Here, Schultz describes the defendants' "tacit understanding" of a shared goal. Schultz also dismisses the long efforts to se-

cure permits and the talk of nonviolence as a ploy to entice unwitting demonstrators into a violent confrontation with police.

[Document Source: *The Conspiracy Trial*, eds., Judy Clavir and John Spitzer (Indianapolis, IN: Bobbs-Merrill Co., 1970), 552–53.]

Let me briefly discuss the conspiracy charge.

We have shown that these defendants, all seven of them, had a mutual understanding to accomplish the objects of the conspiracy, that they had a common purpose of bringing disruption and inciting a violence in this city, and that all seven of them together participated in working together and siding each other to further these plans. Oh, they never explicitly said, "You do that to blow up that," and "I will do that to incite that crowd," that is not how they did it. It was tacit understanding, a working together in all these meetings and all of these conferences that they had, and that is how they conspired.

The only difference between five of the defendants and the remaining two, Rubin and Hoffman, were the ways of getting the people here. Rubin and Hoffman were going to get their people here by a music festival, and the others were going to get their people here by saying they were going to have a counter-convention of the grassroots of America.

All seven defendants worked together jointly for the common purpose and discussed and planned together for the common purpose of creating violent conflict and disruptions in this city. They were going to incite violence in this city by bringing other people here and by coming here themselves. We have proven the defendants guilty on the substantive counts as well as the conspiracy charge, as we charge.

The last area I want to cover are march permits. Most of Davis' direct examination was to impress you on how genuinely he tried to get march permits and an assembly site at the Amphitheatre. Well, he wanted a march permit and he wanted an assembly permit at the Amphitheatre, but it doesn't follow that because he wanted permits he wanted to avoid violence. Don't be fooled by that. Why did Davis want permits for the Amphitheatre? He wanted permits first to make it look like "We are trying to avoid violence. We want permits."

Number two, he wanted permits because they wanted to be where the TV cameras were, at the Amphitheatre.

And, number three, they wanted permits because they wanted the confrontation right at the Amphitheatre, right at the Amphitheatre.

Leonard Weinglass, closing argument for the defendants, February 12, 1970

In his closing arguments, Defense Attorney Leonard Weinglass sought to undermine the prosecution's definition of a conspiracy and to challenge the testimony of government witnesses who claimed the defendants spoke of plans for violence. He then finished by asserting that the trial was a government effort to suppress dissent and that the defendants were in a long tradition of defenders of liberty. When Weinglass sought to link the prosecution to the Salem witch trials and the persecution of Jesus, the U.S. attorney had had enough, and Judge Hoffman upheld the government's objection. Weinglass's remarks were part of a sustained effort to convince the jury of the political character of the trial and to emphasize the historical importance of the outcome.

[Document Source: *The Conspiracy Trial*, eds., Judy Clavir and John Spitzer (Indianapolis, IN: Bobbs-Merrill Co., 1970), 561–62.]

It seems to me that if the lesson of the country teaches anything, it is that the true patriots are the people who take a position on principle and hold to it, and if there are people in this country who feel that the people in Vietnam are not our enemies, but another part of the humanity on this planet against whom this country is transgressing, and they take action, peaceful action, to protest their feeling, like Abe Lincoln did 120 years ago, there is nothing terribly unpatriotic about it, and rather than to derive from hatred for their country, it seems to me to derive from love of country, and these people have always had it difficult.

When Dave Dellinger and Tom Hayden and Rennie Davis, all men in the peace movement, stated shortly after the Convention, "We have won, we have won," Mr. Schultz attempts to indicate to you that what they were talking about is that they have won in their plans to have violence.

I submit to you that the more reasonable interpretation of that is that people in the United States have won and the peace movement has won because people stood up for a principle, they stood up for what they thought was right. They were beaten and struck down in the streets. They were gassed in the park. But far from defeat, they stood, and they stood their ground. What happened here in Chicago during the week of the Convention is an unfortunate incident on the record of this country. But like all other wrongs that have happened, they can be righted only by people who are willing to stand up to the wrong and embrace the truth and the justice that they see and to stand by what they believe to be true.

I submit to you this task is now before you, and whether this wrong, which is the prosecution of those who were the victims of official misconduct and are brought to trial in an attempt to justify that conduct, is ever righted, resides solely and exclusively in your province.

Throughout history it has always been easy to go along. They did it at the Salem witch trials. They went along in Jerusalem—

Mr. Schultz: Oh, objection, if the Court please.

The Court: I see no relationship of the Salem witch trials to this courtroom. I don't think it is comparable. I sustain the objection.

Mr. Weinglass: I merely want to indicate to you in finishing that this case is more than just the defense of seven men. It involves the more basic issue of whether or not those who stand up to dare can do so without grave personal risk and I think it will be judged in that light, and I think while you deliberate this case, that history will hold its breath until you determine whether or not this wrong that we have been living with will be righted by a verdict of acquittal for the seven men who are on trial here.

Thank you.

William Kunstler, closing argument for the defendants, February 13, 1970

Kunstler took one last opportunity to argue that the defendants were being prosecuted for their political beliefs, and he set the case in a broad historical context of political martyrs.

[Document Source: *The Conspiracy Trial*, eds., Judy Clavir and John Spitzer (Indianapolis, IN: Bobbs-Merrill Co., 1970), 567.]

We are living in extremely troubled times, as Mr. Weinglass pointed out. An intolerable war abroad has divided and dismayed us all. Racism at home and poverty at home are both causes of despair and discouragement. In a so-called affluent society, we have people starving and people who can't even begin to approximate the decent life.

These are rough problems, terrible problems, and as has been said by everybody in this country, they are so enormous that they stagger the imagination. But they don't go away by destroying their critics. They don't vanish by sending men to jail. They never did and they never will.

To use these problems by attempting to destroy those who protest against them is probably the most indecent thing that we can do. You can crucify a Jesus, you can poison a Socrates, you can hang John Brown or Nathan Hale, you can kill a Che Guevara, you can jail a Eugene Debs or a Bobby Seale. You can assassinate John Kennedy or a Martin Luther King, but the problems remain. The solutions are essentially made by continuing and perpetuating with every breath you have the right of men to think, the right of men to speak boldly and unafraid, the right to be masters of their souls, the right to live free and to die free. The hangman's rope never solved a single problem except that of one man.

I think if this case does nothing else, perhaps it will bring into focus that again we are in that moment of history when a courtroom becomes the proving ground of whether we do live free and whether we do die free. You are in that position now. Suddenly all importance has shifted to you—shifted to you as I guess in the last analysis it should go, and it is really your responsibility, I think, to see that men remain able to think, to speak boldly and unafraid, to be masters of their souls, and to live and die free. And perhaps if you do what is right, perhaps Allen Ginsberg will never have to write again as he did in "Howl," "I saw the best minds of my generation destroyed by madness," perhaps Judy Collins will never have to stand in any courtroom again and say as she did, "When will they ever learn? When will they ever learn?"

U.S. Attorney Thomas Foran, closing argument for the government, February 13, 1970

For the lead prosecutor, the professed political concerns of the defendants were no more than "bunk." Thomas Foran portrayed the organizers of the demonstrations as fomenters of social chaos. In its decision reversing the criminal convictions of five of the defendants, the U.S. Court of Appeals for the Seventh Circuit would cite Foran's closing remarks as evidence of his unacceptable prejudice against the defendants.

[Document Source: *The Conspiracy Trial*, eds., Judy Clavir and John Spitzer (Indianapolis, IN: Bobbs-Merrill Co., 1970), 572.]

What is their intent? And this is their own words: "To disrupt. To pin delegates in the Convention hall. To clog streets. To force the use of troops. To have actions so militant the Guard will have to be used. To have war in the streets until there is peace in Vietnam. To intimidate the establishment so much it will smash the city. Thousands and thousands of people perform disruptive actions in Chicago. Tear this city apart. Fuck up the Convention. Send them out. We'll start the revolution now. Do they want to fight? The United States is an outlaw nation which had broken all the rules so peace demonstrators can break all the rules. Violate all the laws. Go to jail. Disrupt the United States Government in every way that you can. See you in Chicago."

And these men would have you believe that the issue in this case is whether or not they really wanted permits.

Public authority is supposed to stand handcuffed and mute in the face of people like that and say, "We will let you police yourselves"? How would public authority feel if they let that park be full of young kids through that Convention with no policemen, with no one watching them? What about the rape and the bad trips and worse that public authority would be responsible for if it had?

They tried to give us this bunk that they wanted to talk about racism and the war and they wanted a counter-convention. They didn't do anything but look for a confrontation with the police. What they looked for was a fight, and all that permits had to do with it was where was the fight going to be, and that's all.

And they are sophisticated and they are smart and they are well-educated. And they are as evil as they can be.

Judge Hoffman, charge to the jury, February 14, 1970

Judge Hoffman reminded the jurors of several key points of law that had often been lost in the turmoil of the trial. Recent Supreme Court decisions, such as Brandenburg v. Ohio, had expanded the First Amendment protections of speech that merely advocated illegal action but that was not directly connected to promoting or encouraging that illegal action. Hoffman also informed the jury that the First Amendment protected public assembly without a normally required permit if the individuals organizing the assembly made a reasonable effort to obtain a permit. The jurors were left to decide if the prosecution had established beyond any reasonable doubt that the defendants had intended to incite violence and had taken action to promote that violence.

[Document Source: *The Conspiracy Trial*, eds., Judy Clavir and John Spitzer (Indianapolis, IN: Bobbs-Merrill Co., 1970), 576.]

Ladies and gentlemen of the jury, I shall now instruct you as to what kind of conduct is not prohibited by law, and cannot, therefore, constitute grounds for conviction.

Among the most vital and precious liberties which we Americans enjoy by virtue of our Constitution are freedom of speech and freedom of assembly. The freedoms guaranteed by the First Amendment allow criticism of existing institutions, of political leaders, of domestic and foreign policies and our system of government. That right is unaffected by whether or not it may seem to you to be wrong, intemperate or offensive or designed to undermine public confidence in existing government.

The law distinguishes between mere advocacy of violence or lawlessness without more, and advocacy of the use of force or illegality where such advocacy is directed to inciting, promoting, or encouraging lawless actions. The Constitution does not protect speech which is reasonably and knowingly calculated and directed to inciting actions which violate the law. A conviction can rest only on advocacy which constitutes a call to imminent unlawful action.

You must keep in mind this distinction between constitutionally protected and unprotected speech.

In addition it is a constitutional exercise of the rights of free speech and assembly to march or hold a rally without a permit where applications for permits were made in good faith at a reasonable time prior to the date of march or rally and the permits were denied arbitrarily or discriminatorily.

Where the law refers to an act that is committed knowingly and willfully, it means that the act was done voluntarily and purposely, not because of mistake or accident, with knowledge that it was prohibited by law and with the purpose of violating the law. Thus the defendants cannot be found to have acted willfully and knowingly unless they or any of them did so with a bad purpose of an evil intent. Such knowledge and intent may be proven by the defendants' conduct and by all of the facts and circumstances of the case as shown by the evidence.

If you are not convinced beyond a reasonable doubt that a defendant acted knowingly and willfully, then you must find that the Government has failed to prove the intent necessary and you must, in such an event, acquit that defendant.

U.S. Court of Appeals for the Seventh Circuit, decision on the defendants' appeal of the contempt convictions, May 11, 1972

The court of appeals dismissed some of the contempt convictions against the defense attorneys and reversed all other contempt convictions of the attorneys as well as the defendants. In this excerpt from the opinion written by Judge Walter Cummings, the court of appeals addressed the acceptable behavior of attorneys. While acknowledging that the trial judge must have ultimate authority to regulate behavior in the courtroom, the court of appeals said that a trial judge cannot punish an attorney for reasonable persistence in advocating a client's case. The court also rejected Judge Hoffman's assumption that an attorney should be held responsible for the courtroom behavior of a client.

[Document Source: *In re* Dellinger et al., 461 F.2d 389 (1972).]

And where the judge is arbitrary or affords counsel inadequate opportunity to argue his position, counsel must be given substantial leeway in pressing his contention, for it is through such colloquy that the judge may recognize his mistake and prevent error from infecting the record. It is, after all, the full intellectual exchange of ideas and positions that best facilitates the resolution of disputes. However, this is not to say that attorneys may press their positions beyond the court's insistent direction to desist. On the contrary, the necessity for orderly administration of justice compels the view that the judge must have the power to set limits on argument. We simply encourage judges to exercise tolerance in determining those limits and to distinguish carefully between hesitating, begrudging obedience and open defiance.

A reading of the specifications against the attorneys in this case reveals a pattern in the specifications for refusal to obey a court directive to cease argument. That pattern necessitates a brief comment. The record discloses that the trial judge, when ordering counsel to terminate their argument or sit down, frequently added a rejoinder or coupled the order with a statement which called for a response by the attorneys. In such situations, it is our view that an invited, additional response cannot subsequently be viewed as a contemptuous violation of the order.....

Yet another frequent charge against the attorneys is that they failed to aid the court in maintaining order. While this charge was often coupled with the additional assertion that they actively encouraged their clients in their disruptions, for purposes of remand it is necessary to distinguish between the two situations. An attorney has no affirmative obligation to restrain his client under pain of the contempt sanction, although we do not express an opinion as to the breach of professional ethics that may be involved in this situation. Indeed, compelling an attorney to control the conduct of his client under threat of the contempt sanction might well destroy the confidence in the attorney–client relationship which is necessary to a proper and adequate defense. However, where an attorney encourages disruptive behavior by a client or fans the flames of existing frictions, he cannot find immunity from punishment for such conduct.

U.S. Court of Appeals for the Seventh Circuit, decision on the defendants' appeal of the criminal convictions, November 21, 1972

> *The U.S. Court of Appeals for the Seventh Circuit reversed the criminal convictions of the five defendants and remanded the cases for retrial at the government's discretion. In the opinion written by Judge Thomas Fairchild, the court of appeals addressed the defendants' arguments in favor of various grounds for reversal, including the constitutionality of the Anti-Riot Act, the composition of the grand jury and the selection of the petit jury, the trial judge's rulings on the admissibility of evidence and testimony of witnesses, the undisclosed communications between the judge and the jury, and the demeanor of the judge and the prosecuting attorneys. The court by a vote of 2–1 upheld the constitutionality of the Anti-Riot Act, but it found other grounds for reversal.*

[Document Source: United States v. Dellinger, 472 F.2d 340 (1972).]

Constitutionality of the Anti-Riot Act

The first amendment is premised upon the value of unfettered speech. Constitutional protection is clearly not to be limited, therefore, to mild or innocuous presentation, and it is unrewarding to search for a formula describing punishable advocacy of violence in terms of fervor or vigor. The real question is whether particular speech is intended to and has such capacity to propel action that it is reasonable to treat such speech as action.

The test for the attributes which speech in favor of violent action must achieve before it may be classified as action and thus removed from first amendment protection has been variously phrased—clear and present danger—directed to inciting and likely to incite imminent lawless action—whether the harm sought by expression is immediate and instantaneous and irremediable except by punishing the expression and thereby preventing the conduct—whether the expression is inseparably locked with action.

Our question, in examining the validity of the Anti-riot Act on its face is whether, properly construed, it punishes speech only when a sufficiently close relationship between such speech and violent action is found to exist. Semantically the cases suggest that while a statutory prohibition of advocacy of violence is overbroad, since protected speech is included within advocacy, a prohibition of intentional incitement of violence is not overbroad. The latter depends upon a construction of "incitement" which is sufficiently likely to propel the violent action to be identified with action. . . . It seems to us that the threshold definition of all categories as "urging or instigating" puts a sufficient gloss of propulsion on the expression described that it can be carved away from the comprehensive protection of the first amendment's guarantee of freedom of speech.

Jury Selection

In evaluating this topic, it is important to recall the time when this trial occurred, and to recognize that the division in public attitudes toward the Vietnam war has changed and is changing still. The extent of unpopularity of the war in 1972, when this opinion is written, is not a fair index of the probable opinions on that subject in a cross section selected in September, 1969. Perspective is important. These defendants' plans for activities in Chicago in August, 1968 were first formed when President Johnson was expected to be a candidate to succeed himself. He withdrew March 31, 1968. The 1968 candidacies of Senators Eugene McCarthy and Robert Kennedy, the latter assassinated in June, 1968, were associated with anti-war sentiment. Further crystallization of anti-war sentiment is associated with the Cambodian venture and the Kent State killings, both in the spring of 1970. These episodes had not yet occurred when the jury was selected for this trial in September, 1969. We have no doubt that defendants brought to trial in 1969 upon charges that their anti-war activities were carried beyond constitutional protection were entitled to a testing of their jurors for biased attitudes on this subject.

Perhaps secondary, but significant, were the conflicts of values represented by the so-called youth culture—hippies, yippies and freaks—in contrast with the more traditional values of the vast majority of the community, presumably including most citizens summoned for jury service. Again, we are not unaware that many otherwise qualified members of the community could not be impartial toward, and in fact are often offended by, persons who wear long hair, beards, and bizarre clothing and who seem to avoid the burdens and responsibilities of regular employment. Several defendants would exemplify this conflict.

A similar conflict of values was symbolized in the confrontation between the city police and the demonstrators. A juror's basic sympathies with the actors in these events could easily impair his ability to consider alternative views of the case as presented in court. A venireman's relationship with law enforcement officers would be an important factor to be inquired about in evaluating his ability to be an impartial juror.

In our view, some minimal inquiry into at least these three basic areas was essential to a fair trial of this extraordinary case, at least when defendants requested such inquiry. . . .

These cases demonstrate the danger that widespread publicity about highly dramatic events will render prospective jurors incapable of impartial consideration of the evidence. We think it must follow that where pretrial publicity is of a character and extent to raise a real probability that veniremen have heard and formed opinions about the events relevant to a case, and at least where, as here, the defense has brought the pretrial publicity to the court's attention and requested voir dire inquiry, the court must make inquiry adequate to determine whether anyone has read or heard about the facts, and, if so, what the impact has been on his ability to serve as an impartial juror.

Demeanor of the Judge and Prosecutors

The district judge's deprecatory and often antagonistic attitude toward the defense is evident in the record from the very beginning. It appears in remarks and actions both in the presence and absence of the jury.

The defense presented an extensive case, calling more than 100 witnesses. The judge might, within reason, have alleviated some of the difficulties defense counsel encountered, but he did not do so.

There are a number of areas in the law of evidence in which lawyers and judges differ considerably in interpretation of the rules and where the application of a rule is really governed by the discretion or individual views of the trial judge. When a question is leading; when testimony that another person made a statement is admissible because the making of the statement is relevant, even though the statement also contains assertions of fact; when a question on cross-examination is outside the scope of the direct; when a question is objectionable because repetitive—are all examples of such areas. We shall not attempt the task of reviewing all the rulings on evidence in this case. It does appear, however, that in comparable situations, the judge was more likely to exercise his discretion against the defense than against the government.

Most significant, however, were remarks in the presence of the jury, deprecatory of defense counsel and their case. These comments were often touched with sarcasm, implying rather than saying outright that defense counsel was inept, bumptious, or untrustworthy, or that his case lacked merit. Sometimes the comment was not associated with any ruling in ordinary course; sometimes gratuitously added to an otherwise proper ruling; nearly always unnecessary. Taken individually any one was not very significant and might be disregarded as a harmless attempt at humor. But cumulatively, they must have telegraphed to the jury the judge's contempt for the defense. . . .

In final argument, the United States Attorney went at least up to, and probably beyond, the outermost boundary of permissible inferences from the evidence in his characterizations of defendants. He referred to them as "evil men," "liars and obscene haters," "profligate extremists," and "violent anarchists." He suggested one defendant was doing well as it got dark because "predators always operate better when it gets close to dark."

He yielded to the temptation to exploit the courtroom conduct of various defendants which formed the basis of the contempt citations in *In re Dellinger*. He told the jurors they need not ignore "how those people look and act," "outbursts in the courtroom," "the sudden respect, the sudden decency" occurring "in the last few days as we reach the end of the case," the suggested similarity between the technique the jurors had seen used in the courtroom with the marshals and that allegedly used at the time of the convention with the police.

Dress, personal appearance, and conduct at trial were not probative of guilt. The district judge properly instructed the jurors that they "must not in any way be influenced by any possible antagonism you may have toward the defendants or any of them, their dress, hair styles, speech, reputation, courtroom demeanor or quality, personal philosophy or life style." The United States Attorney should not have urged the jury to consider those things.

We conclude that the demeanor of the judge and prosecutors would require reversal if other errors did not.

Judge Edward Gignoux, decision on the retrial of the contempt convictions—comments on the proper conduct of a trial, December 6, 1973

Judge Gignoux presided over the retrial of the remaining contempt charges against the defendants and their attorneys. After his meticulous review of the contempt specifications and his rejection of all but thirteen of them, Gignoux addressed the impact of Judge Hoffman's management of the case and the general purpose of rules governing courtroom behavior. Gignoux was most concerned with ensuring public confidence in a fair and impartial trial process.

[Document Source: *In re* David T. Dellinger et al., 370 F. Supp. 1304, 1321–23.]

From the foregoing, it is apparent that the contumacious conduct of the defendants and their lawyers cannot be considered apart from the conduct of the trial judge and prosecutors. Each reacted to provocation by the other, and the tensions generated during four and a half months of so acrimonious a trial cannot be ignored. Indeed, with the exception of the two specifications relating to the "robe" incident . . . , the contumacious conduct of the four remaining defendants can, in each instance, reasonably be said to have been in response, albeit an excessive response, to peremptory action of the judge.

Present government counsel urge that substantial jail sentences for these defendants are necessary to vindicate the judicial process and to deter other defendants and defense counsel from similar misbehavior. After a careful evaluation of the record, however, this Court is convinced that, in the particular circumstances here present, the affirmation of the integrity of trial proceedings and the goal of deterrence have both been achieved by the findings of guilt. The Court is further persuaded that, at this late date, four years after the events which gave rise to these charges, no warrant exists for the imposition of jail sentences additional to the periods of imprisonment which have already been served by the non-lawyer defendants. While Mr. Kunstler was never incarcerated, in the considered judgment of the Court, no purpose, other than the impermissible purpose of vindictiveness, would be served by sentencing him to prison at this time. The condemnation of his conduct and the potentially grave consequences of a criminal contempt conviction to a member of the bar should serve as adequate deterrents to other lawyers who may be disposed to similar misbehavior.

In light of the unique character and long history of this case, and the defendants' attack on the integrity and fairness of the American judicial process, a concluding observation is appropriate. Throughout these proceedings, the defense has asserted that both the 1969 Anti-Riot Act prosecution and the present contempt proceedings have been "political trials" designed to suppress dissent. This position, they claim, gives them license unilaterally to dispense with the standards of civility to which American lawyers and litigants customarily adhere in criminal, as well as civil, trials. It is precisely to preserve the opportunity for the fair and dispassionate resolution of strenuously contested disputes by an impartial tribunal that rules governing the behavior of all the actors in a trial exist. . . .

Trials which proceed in accordance with the law, the rules of evidence and the standards of demeanor not only reaffirm the integrity and viability of the judicial process, but also serve to insure the ability of each one of us to protect the rights and liberties we enjoy as citizens.

Anti-Riot Act

The Chicago conspiracy trial defendants were the first individuals prosecuted under the anti-riot provisions that Congress incorporated in the Civil Rights Act of 1968. The U.S. House of Representatives in 1967 overwhelmingly passed a version of the anti-riot provision in response to the urban riots of that summer and assertions from some members of Congress that African-American political activists had instigated the violence. The Senate included the provision in an open housing bill, and although President Johnson and Attorney General Ramsey Clark did not support the anti-riot provision, the administration accepted it to secure passage of the civil rights measure.

[Document Source: 82 Stat. 75.]

2101. Riots

(a) (1) Whoever travels in interstate or foreign commerce or uses any facility of interstate or foreign commerce or uses any facility of interstate or foreign commerce, including, but not limited to, the mail, telegraph, telephone, radio, or television, with intent –

(A) to incite a riot; or (B) to organize, promote, encourage, participate in, or carry on a riot; or (C) to commit any act of violence in furtherance of a riot; or (D) to aid or abet any person in inciting or participating in or carrying on a riot or committing any act of violence in furtherance of a riot; and who either during the course of any such travel or use or thereafter performs or attempts to perform any other overt act for any purpose specified in subparagraph (A), (B), (C), or (D) of this paragraph shall be fined not more than $10,000, or imprisoned not more than five years, or both. (b) In any prosecution under this section, proof that a defendant engaged or attempted to engage in one or more of the overt acts described in subparagraph (A), (B), (C), or (D) of paragraph (1) of subsection (a) and (1) has traveled in interstate or foreign commerce, or (2) has use of or used any facility of interstate or foreign commerce, including but not limited to, mail, telegraph, telephone, radio, or television, to communicate with or broadcast to any person or group of persons prior to such overt acts, such travel or use shall be admissible proof to establish that such defendant traveled in or used such facility of interstate or foreign commerce.

"The Strategy of Confrontation," report of the Daley administration

Mayor Daley ordered his administration and the city police to prepare a report that would correct what Daley characterized as "unfortunate, inaccurate reporting." The report, quickly drafted under the direction of city counsel Raymond Simon, insisted that the police had been restrained in the face of revolutionary violence, and it offered statistics on the relatively small number of arrests and injuries. The report blamed the violence on the actions of a small group of political activists, and specifically cited Rennie Davis, Tom Hayden, Abbie Hoffman, Jerry Rubin, and David Dellinger, whose brief biographies showed "that they are not strangers to the tactics of confrontation." The American Civil Liberties Union called the report "utterly dishonest." At a press conference displaying confiscated weapons, including a jarred black widow spider, police superintendent James Conlisk announced that in the future the Chicago police would use more tear gas to control mobs.

[Document Source: "The Strategy of Confrontation: Chicago and the Democratic National Convention – 1968." Report prepared by Raymond F. Simon, corporation counsel, City of Chicago, Sept. 6, 1968, pp. 49–50.]

Conclusion

The leaders of the dissident movement are nationally known agitators who had arrived fresh from triumphs at Berkeley and Columbia. Their publicly stated purpose in coming to Chicago was twofold. The immediate object was to disrupt the Convention and the City. Their ultimate goal, also publicly proclaimed, was to topple what they consider to be the corrupt institutions of our society, educational, governmental, etc., by impeding and if possible halting their normal functions while exposing the authorities to ridicule and embarrassment. They are anxious to destroy these institutions, but it is unclear as to what replacements they envision, as Senator Daniel Inouye of Hawaii observed in the Convention's Keynote address when he asked "what trees do they plant?"

The dual goals of immediate disruption and ultimate destruction were pursued in Chicago against the government under the guise of a protest against the war in Vietnam. This promised to be a very successful ploy since, as debates at the Convention demonstrated, everyone wants peace and disagreement occurs only over methods.

In spite of such attractive bait, the guerilla or psychological warfare tactics which were employed by these revolutionaries erupted in few serious incidents, the main one being an eighteen minute encounter in front of the Hilton Hotel. As is so often the case, the trusting, the innocent, and the idealist were taken in and taken over. The news media, too, responded with surprising naivete and were incredibly misused. Indeed, any success the revolutionaries achieved in their ultimate objectives of fomenting hatred and ridicule among the citizenry against the authorities was in large part attributable to the almost totally sympathetic coverage extended by reporters to the revolutionary leaders and more understandably, to the attractive idealistic but unwary young people who unwittingly lent them assistance and camouflage. . . .

It seems clear that a nucleus of adult trouble makers avowedly seeking a hostile confrontation with the police will be engaging in the same activities detailed in this report in other cities and towns across the nation. They have announced their intention "to create 200 to 300 Chicagos." All who believe in the essential desirability of our present form of government are challenged to find the best response to what is frequently a violent and revolutionary attack upon our institutions—a response at once effective yet consistent with the dignity and freedom of each and all our citizens.

Walker Report summary

On September 4, 1968, Milton Eisenhower, chair of the National Commission on the Causes and Prevention of Violence, announced that the commission would investigate the violence at the Chicago convention and report its findings to President Lyndon Johnson. A Chicago lawyer, Daniel Walker, headed the team of over 200 members, who interviewed more than 1,400 witnesses to the events and studied FBI reports and film of the confrontations. The report released on December 1, 1968, characterized the convention violence as a "police riot" and recommended prosecution of police who used indiscriminate violence. The report made clear that the vast majority of police had behaved responsibly, but it said that failure to prosecute the police who misbehaved would further damage public confidence in law enforcement. Chief Judge William Campbell criticized the release of the report before the completion of the grand jury investigation and suggested that the grand jury might need to investigate the motivation for the release. Milton Eisenhower, however, defended the commission's decision to publish the report because of "widespread interest" in the findings. The report was unvarnished in its presentation of the language used by demonstrators and their provocation of the police, but it also blamed the violence on the city government's refusal to allow permits.

[Document Source: Rights in Conflict. Convention Week in Chicago, August 25–29, 1968. A Report submitted by Daniel Walker, Director of the Chicago Study Team, to the National Commission on the Causes and Prevention of Violence. Introduction by Max Frankel. New York: E.P. Dutton, 1968. pp. 1, 10–11.]

A Summary

During the week of the Democratic National Convention, the Chicago police were the targets of mounting provocation by both word and act. It took the form of obscene epithets, and of rocks, sticks, bathroom tiles and even human feces hurled at police by demonstrators. Some of these acts had been planned; others were spontaneous or were themselves provoked by police action. Furthermore, the police had been put on edge by widely published threats of attempts to disrupt both the city and the Convention.

That was the nature of the provocation. The nature of the response was unrestrained and indiscriminate police violence on many occasions, particularly at night.

That violence was made all the more shocking by the fact that it was often inflicted upon persons who had broken no law, disobeyed no order, made no threat. These included peaceful demonstrators, onlookers, and large numbers of residents who were simply passing through, or happened to live in, the areas where confrontations were occurring.

Newsmen and photographers were singled out for assault, and their equipment deliberately damaged. Fundamental police training was ignored; and officers, when on the scene, were often unable to control their men. As one police officer put it: "What happened didn't have anything to do with police work." . . .

Police violence was a fact of convention week. Were the policemen who committed it a minority? It appears certain that they were—but one which has imposed some of the consequences of its actions on the majority, and certainly on their commanders. There has been no public condemnation of these violators of sound police procedures and common decency by either their commanding officers or city officials. Nor (at the time this Report is being completed—almost three months after the convention) has any disciplinary action been taken against most of them. That some policemen lost control of themselves under exceedingly provocative circumstances can perhaps be understood; but not condoned. If no action is taken against them, the effect can only be to discourage the majority of policemen who acted responsibly, and further weaken the bond between police and community.

Although the crowds were finally dispelled on the nights of violence in Chicago, the problems they represent have not been. Surely this is not the last time that a violent dissenting group will clash head-on with those whose duty it is to enforce the law. And the next time the whole world will still be watching.

The committee to defend the conspiracy

A committee of notable writers, academics, and performers published this call for financial support of the defendants as they approached the start of the trial. The committee warned that the indictment was part of a government effort to silence political dissent and warned that prosecutions under the Anti-Riot Act, which criminalized intent rather than actions, would lead to a "police state." The committee saw the trial as an opportunity to educate the public about the issues that had brought the demonstrators to the Chicago convention. A week before this letter was published, Rennie Davis held a press conference in Chicago to announce fundraising for the legal fees. The defendants now referred to themselves as "The Conspiracy" and they

planned meetings across the country to educate the public about the impending trial
and "to raise questions of who are the criminals in America today."
[Document Source: *New York Review of Books*, v. 12, n. 12 (June 19, 1969).]

The federal indictment in Chicago of eight political dissenters for conspiracy to promote disorder and riot during the week of the Democratic National Convention is one of the most ominous challenges to political liberty since the passing of Senator Joseph R. McCarthy. It calls for a clear and considered response from all who believe that the preservation of political dissent is now, more than ever, crucial to the survival of democratic process in America.

. . . We are now organizing a large group of sponsors for a national campaign built around the following statement:

"Eight political activists who were prominent in the mass demonstrations of protest during the Democratic National Convention in Chicago are now under federal indictment for criminal conspiracy. They are the first persons to be so charged under Title 18 of the Civil Rights Act of 1968 which makes it a felony to "travel in interstate commerce . . . with the intent to incite, promote, encourage, participate in and carry on a riot. . . ."

"The effect of this 'anti-riot' act is to subvert the first Amendment guarantee of free assembly by equating organized political protest with organized violence. Potentially, this law is the foundation for a police state in America.

"In this decade, countless Americans have contributed to the revitalization of politics through freedom rides, peace marches and other demonstrations of protest against impacted political institutions. Yet, from Bull Connor's Birmingham to Richard Daley's Chicago, civil authorities have employed police violence to suppress 'the right of the people peaceably to assemble,' repeatedly invoking the specters of conspiracy, incitement and riot. The Justice Department has now joined the assault on free political action.

"Title 18, the 'anti-riot' provision, was attached to the Civil Rights Act of 1968 by a repressive coalition in the Congress and was aimed at black civil rights activists. Enacted in the wake of the urban riots that followed the murder of Martin Luther King, the rider found support even among members of the Congress who might ordinarily resist the delusion that social disorder is the sinister work of 'outside agitators.'

"The 'anti-riot' clause and the indictment in Chicago are legally and Constitutionally dubious. While *acts* of violence, incitement and disruption are explicitly covered by numerous, long-established state and local laws, conspiracy—which deals not with act but with intent—is a vague concept at best. Prosecution for conspiracy requires no proof of the commission of a crime, nor even of an attempt. Thus the prosecution of conspiracy all too easily becomes political harassment of persons who hold dissenting ideas.

"It is especially surprising that this new law should first be tested in connection with the Chicago disorders. For the events of convention week do reveal, with terrible clarity, that it is local authority and police who decide whether violence attends civil demonstration. In this case, the responsibility of the Chicago authorities is the more striking when it is remembered that several of the eight men under indictment have helped to organize major public demonstrations in other cities, both before and after the week of the Democratic National Convention. None of these demonstrations resulted in riot. . . .

"Confronted by a patently political challenge, the eight defendants have determined on a political response as well as a legal defense. Through their trial they will carry forward the first constitutional challenge to the anti-riot act. They intend, as well, to refocus public attention on the root issues that brought them and thousands of others to Chicago and the Democratic National Convention—the war, racism, the widening power of the military-academic-industrial complex, the enfeeblement of the nation's political process. As a sign of their refusal to be intimidated by the scare label the government would hang upon them, the defendants are calling themselves *The Conspiracy*; and they are inviting other Americans who are similarly committed to radical change in this nation to join *The Conspiracy*. They are also appealing for financial and moral support to Americans who find in this indictment disturbing implications for the safeguard of constitutional liberty and a democratic political life. . . .

Peter Babcox, Noam Chomsky, Judy Collins, Harvey Cox, Edgar Z. Friedenberg, Michael Harrington, Nat Hentoff, Donald Kalish, Christopher Lasch, Sidney Lens, Herbert Magidson, Norman Mailer, Stewart Meacham, Larry David Nachman, Conor Cruise O'Brien, Susan Sontag, Benjamin Spock, I. F. Stone, Harold Taylor

Tom Wicker, "'Other Thoughts' in Chicago"

Like many journalists covering the Chicago conspiracy trial, Tom Wicker noted that the proceedings often bore little resemblance to other criminal trials. In addition to the colorful witnesses and the theatrical behavior of the judge and defendants, the charge faced by the defendants, according to Wicker, bore little resemblance to other criminal charges and raised fundamental questions about the fairness of the law.
[Document Source: "In the Nation" column, *New York Times*, Jan. 22, 1970.]

An air of unreality hangs over the trial of the so-called "Chicago Seven," and not merely because it keeps turning up such witnesses as Country Joe, the leader of the rock group known as Country Joe and the Fish.

Bearded, wearing an Indian headband and purple boots, he gave his name as Country Joe. And when the prosecution demanded full identification, Judge Julius Hoffman replied in tones of resignation: "Well, I assume his Christian name must be 'Country.'"

But again, it is not just Judge Hoffman's undeniable theatrical gifts nor even the widespread belief—given frequent official voice by the defense counsel—that he favors the prosecution, that makes this landmark trial seem so alien to a conventional assumption of the fitness of things.

Issue Obscured

It is more nearly because there is so little talk or testimony about any of the familiar events that might be thought to be at issue. Surprisingly little is being said about the actual events that surrounded the Democratic convention of 1968, the marches, the police response, the violence in the streets, and although echoes of grim nights in Grant Park keep coming through—their vibrations were certainly bad, as Country Joe put it—the testimony here is focused elsewhere, and rather hazily at that....

And that in the final analysis is why this sometimes ludicrous proceeding seems to have so little relationship, not only just to what happened in Chicago in August of 1968, but to any of our familiar notions of what trials are all about, of what constitutes legal guilt, of what the law's limits are in America.

The Chicago Seven are not being tried for committing acts of violence in August of 1968; nor are they even being tried for having *caused* the violence that did take place.

They are, rather, charged with "conspiring" to disrupt the convention with violence, and it is this "conspiracy"—whether it existed—that is the issue in Judge Hoffman's court. It is at least theoretically possible, therefore, that even had there been no violence at all, the Seven could still be on trial here for taking part in the alleged conspiracy.

Intentions as Cause

Violence did, of course, take place in Chicago in August, 1968. It may be that some, or all of the defendants intended or hoped for violence. But the intention, on the one hand, did not necessarily cause the violence, on the other. If the Seven were on trial here to determine whether acts or intentions of theirs did cause the convention-week violence that actually happened, there would be only a factual question of guilt or innocence to be determined—the usual business of a criminal trial.

But that is not the case. The defendants here are the first to be tried under a provision of the 1968 Civil Rights Act that made it a Federal crime to cross a state line with the intention to cause a riot or a disturbance. The constitutionality of this statute has yet to be determined, but the Chicago trial clearly suggests—as indeed, does the language of the act—that what it seeks to prohibit or penalize is a state of mind, not an overt act.

Burden of Proof

Ironically, it is also pretty clear from this proceeding how difficult it is to prove a state of mind, long afterwards. It is probably more difficult for the prosecution, on whom rests the burden of proof, than for the defendants, which is why Mr. Schultz sound so preposterous in his efforts to show that Rennie Davis was saying one thing to Roger Wilkins while "thinking other thoughts."

Nevertheless, if the issue of a trial actually comes down to "other thoughts," rather than to actual words and deeds, the deeper question may be whether even "the burden of proof" any longer means anything.

Bibliography

The Conspiracy Trial. Eds., Judy Clavir and John Spitzer. Indianapolis, IN: Bobbs-Merrill Co., 1970.

Danelski, David J. "The Chicago Conspiracy Trial." In Theodore L. Becker, ed. *Political Trials.* Indianapolis, IN: Bobbs-Merrill Co., 1971, 134–80.

Ely, James W., Jr. "The Chicago Conspiracy Case." In Michal R. Belknap, ed. *American Political Trials.* Westport: Greenwood Press, 1981, pp. 233–53.

Epstein, Jason. *The Great Conspiracy Trial: An Essay on Law, Liberty and the Constitution.* New York: Random House, 1970.

Hayden, Tom. *Reunion: A Memoir.* New York: Random House, 1988.

Hayden, Tom. *Trial.* New York: Holt, Rinehart and Winston, 1970.

Hoffman, Abbie. *Soon to be a Major Motion Picture.* New York: Perigee Books, 1980.

Kinoy, Arthur, Helene E. Schwartz & Doris Peterson. *Conspiracy on Appeal: Appellate Brief on Behalf of the Chicago Eight.* New York: Agathon Publication Services, Inc., 1971.

Lahav, Pnina. "Law and Character: Chicago Conspiracy Trial: Character and Judicial Discretion," *University of Colorado Law Review* (2000), 1327.

Lahav, Pnina. "Theater in the Courtroom: The Chicago Conspiracy Trial," *Cardozo Studies in Law and Literature* 16 (Fall 2004), 381.

Lukas, J. Anthony. *The Barnyard Epithet and Other Obscenities: Notes on the Chicago Conspiracy Trial.* New York: Harper and Row, 1970.

Mailer, Norman. *Miami and the Siege of Chicago: An Informal History of the Republican and Democratic Conventions of 1968.* New York: World Publishing, 1968.

Raskin, Jonah. *For the Hell of It: The Life and Times of Abbie Hoffman.* Berkeley: University of California Press, 1996.

Rubin, Jerry. *Growing (Up) at Thirty-seven.* New York: M. Evans and Co., 1976.

Schultz, John. *The Chicago Conspiracy Trial.* New York: DaCapo Press, 1993.

Seale, Bobby. *The Lonely Rage: The Autobiography of Bobby Seale.* New York: Times Books, 1978.

Conspiracy in the Streets: The Extraordinary Trial of the Chicago Eight. Edited with an Introduction by Jon Weiner. New York: The New Press, 2006.

Rights in Conflict. Convention Week in Chicago, August 25–29, 1968. A Report submitted by Daniel Walker, Director of the Chicago Study Team, to the National Commission on the Causes and Prevention of Violence. Introduction by Max Frankel. New York: E.P. Dutton, 1968.